Praise for the original short story
"A Perspective on the Pledge"

Bay of Fundie
http://www.bay-of-fundie.com/archives/298/a-different-perspective-on-the-pledge
December 13, 2007

I just discovered a great short story over at Atheist Ethicist, entitled "A Perspective on the Pledge". It puts the Pledge controversy in a different light. I highly recommend you check it out.

The Daily Doubter:
http://dailydoubt.blogspot.com/2007/12/one-nation-white.html
December 07, 2007

Over at Atheist Ethicist, Alonzo Fyfe has juxtaposed white supremacism onto the Pledge of Allegiance in order to [demonstrate] the wrongness of the phrase under God in it. A truly excellent post that should be read by any justice preparing to rule on the Pledge being recited in schoo'-

Bligbi
http://bligbi.com/2008/02/07/about-that-pledge/
Posted by KC, February 7, 2008

Just a quick note to point out this excellent post by Alonzo Fyfe over at Atheist Ethicist about the loyalty oath here in America.

The Two Percent Company
http://www.twopercentco.com/rants/archives/2006/01/carnival_of_the_18.html
January 22, 2006

One of the posts that we really liked was Alonzo Fyfe's post on Atheist Ethicist entitled A Perspective on the Pledge. It's a great example of using a simple analogy to showcase why the inclusion of "Under God" in the pledge is dead wrong.

Braving the Elements
http://braving-the-elements.blogspot.com/2006/01/wow-cotg-produces-gem-carnival-of.html
January 23, 2006

This one struck home: A Perspective on the Pledge

A PERSPECTIVE ON THE PLEDGE

By Alonzo Fyfe

Earlier versions of the chapters that make up this book first appeared in the
Atheist Ethicist blog (*http://atheistethicist.blogspot.com*)

ISBN: 978-0-6152-0077-4

I owe thanks to John Smith for the cover art, and Marty Mapes for helping me to get this project finished. Diana Hromish and CrypticLife edited earlier drafts of this book. Finally, I owe a debt of gratitude to those who stopped by and left comments on the *Atheist Ethicist* blog where this story first appeared.

For all who have sacrificed to protect and preserve
'one nation, with liberty and justice for all'

Preface

Hello Reader:

The story in this book started off as a blog posting. It was a short story that I wrote to illustrate what it is like sitting in a class while the teacher leads all of the other students in a ritual that effectively says that you are inferior to them and not fit to be included among them.

That is the status of an atheist in America with respect to a Pledge of Allegiance to 'one nation under God' and a motto of 'In God We Trust'.

Clearly, when people pledge allegiance to 'one nation, indivisible' they are saying that patriotic Americans support a *united* states, and those who do not support union are not patriotic Americans. Correspondingly, when people pledge allegiance to one nation with liberty and justice for all they are saying that patriotic Americans support liberty and justice for all, and any who do not support these things cannot be counted as 'one of us' true Americans.

So, when Congress added the phrase 'under God' to the Pledge of Allegiance it was to say that those who would not support a nation under God are like those who would not support union, liberty, or justice. They do not qualify as good, loyal Americans, at least as far as the government is concerned.

What is it like to live in a country where the government's most important lesson to teach in schools and at public events across the country is that you are unworthy of being thought of as 'one of us'? Assume that you have done no wrong, and instead sought always to do what is best for your country and its people. You would even do more for your country and its people if not for the fact that people pledging allegiance to the idea that you are inferior and unfit to be counted as one of them are not prone to put you into a position where you can do more.

The attempt to claim that 'under God' was not meant to promote religion is as absurd as claiming that 'indivisible' was not meant to promote union or that 'with liberty and justice for all' was not meant to promote liberty and justice for all.

Denying that 'under God' was put into the pledge to denigrate and show contempt for those who do not believe in God is a flat-out lie.

More specifically, the words 'under God' were inserted at a time when some people were afraid that those who were not religious might get some measure of political power. Making it the national policy to denigrate those who do not believe in God was the government's way of helping to ensure that power remained in the hands of those who had the 'right' beliefs about God.

The words were inserted to denigrate atheist communists (of the type that lead the Soviet Union). However, with the mindset of true bigots, Congress and President Eisenhower decided that they would condemn all atheists on the basis that some atheists were communists. This is morally equivalent to condemning all blacks on the basis that some blacks use drugs, or condemning all priests because some priests molest children, or condemning all Muslims because some Muslims are terrorists. Or, it would be morally equivalent, if being a communist was equivalent to being a drug addict, child molester, or terrorist. By directing the Pledge and the motto against all atheists, Congress and the President made bigotry the most important value in the country.

In adopting this policy, the government thought that the most important part of teaching this lesson in bigotry was that it be taught to young children – children too young to understand or to question the lesson. Once children this young had been taught that a person has to be 'under God' to be a good American, and that those not 'under God' were bad Americans, the prejudice would be stuck in their minds forever, at least for a large percentage of them.

The truly remarkable thing is that a substantial segment of the population that claims that their religion gives them special access to moral truth has ended up making bigotry the national motto and the national pledge. In denying that this practice promotes hostility towards atheists, they are like the child with pudding all over their face denying that he has eaten any pudding. The lie is that audacious, and it comes from people who claim that their religion has a special power to help them avoid the temptation to do that which is wrong.

A strange fact about a democracy is that, if enough people decide to accept a lie, then the lie can become law. If enough people are willing to vote out of office any legislator who denies that $2 + 2 = 5$, then $2 + 2 = 5$ can get written into the law (much to the detriment of the nation that cares so little about the fact of the matter).

I invented this story to expose the lie behind the Pledge and the Motto. I felt that the story would make the lie that 'pledging allegiance to God is not an act of prejudice against atheists' so obvious that fair-minded people could not ignore it.

I am not suffering from such a delusion that I believe that the story will affect true bigots. Those bigots will probably respond with anger. They will 'misinterpret' the arguments that can be found in this story (or, more commonly, simply assert that the story says things it does not say the way that they assert that the Bible and the Constitution say things they do not say).

Yet, while the bigots are being angry and lying about what I have written, those who actually value justice will be getting a better understanding of what exactly is wrong with having 'under God' in the Pledge of Allegiance. Hopefully, some day, they will find the moral strength to decide to honor their pledge of allegiance to 'justice for all' and correct this moral travesty.

When I posted that original story on my blog, *Atheist Ethicist (http://atheistethicist.blogspot.com)*, the response was quite positive. Then, I found that I could easily expand on the story to explain other wrongs that are imposed on atheists in this country, such as government support for an organization that declares them morally unfit with nothing to support this bigotry but their own prejudice. I could cover enough topics to make the collection of stories into a book – the book that you see before you.

In creating this book, I made some significant changes to the original stories. I weeded out parts that interrupted the flow of the story and added a few more arguments that I thought of after writing the initial posts. Mostly, I edited the separate posts to fit into a coherent story.

I also wanted to include some arguments against having a national motto of 'In God We Trust', since that motto commits the same moral crime as the Pledge as it now stands. Unfortunately, I could not think of a way to write an appropriate analogy into the story that readers would easily understand. Consequently, I put the "In God We Trust" argument at the end of the story in an appendix.

I also want the reader to know that this is not supposed to be literature. I did not write this to entertain, or to present nuanced characters dealing with a difficult situation. This story should be considered more like a Socratic dialogue meant to demonstrate the absurdity, bigotry, and prejudice that sits right on the surface of having a national pledge of allegiance to "one nation under God" and a motto of "In God We Trust."

I also want to point out that, while these issues are typically discussed in terms of 'separation of church and state', I did not want to explore that option, and merely repeat claims that have already been made. I wanted to talk about the difference between right and wrong, not the difference between what is constitutional and what is unconstitutional. If the Constitution actually does not prohibit these acts of bigotry, it is still the case that no fair and just nation would support them. No fair and just nation could support them, since it can be shown that the use of these slogans is both unfair and unjust.

Finally, I wanted to say something about offense and freedom of speech. Some people are going to be offended by what I wrote. Some people are going to interpret this story as saying that my objections to 'under God' and 'In God We Trust' are grounded on my alleged offense at being confronted with mention of God in the public square.

Neither of these interpretations is accurate. I do not consider offense to be morally relevant in itself. A speaker has to be able to say more than that he was offended by a statement in order to justify condemning it. He has to argue that any good person would have been offended.

Some people might also try to claim that a respect for freedom of speech gives people a right to pledge allegiance to 'one nation under God' and to declare, 'In God We Trust'. I want to make it clear that I agree with that statement. However, the right to freedom of speech is not the same as a right to freedom from criticism. The Nazi and the KKK member also have a right to freedom of speech, and even have a right to pledge allegiance to 'one white nation' and to make their motto, 'White Power', if they choose. Their right to freedom of speech is not a right to freedom from condemnation.

So, nothing in this book should be understood as claiming that offense alone is sufficient cause for protesting 'under God' and 'In God We Trust', or that some freedom of speech should be curtailed. Freedom of speech includes the freedom to condemn what others say. We do not have freedom of speech if we do not have the freedom to say, "You are wrong.".

Contents

PREFACE iii

1. And Justice for All 1

2. A Perspective on Scouting..7

3. Patriotism 13

4. Conflicting Duties 19

5. Outside Considerations... 25

6. Jenny.. 31

7. Appeasers 37

8. Hating Ameryca 41

9. Reasons and Causes.. 45

10. Tolerance and Moral Superiority 51

11. The Hearing 59

12. Aftermath.. 65

Appendix A: "In God We Trust".............................. 67

Appendix B: Offense and Freedom of Speech......... 71

1. And Justice for All

Shelby Johnson had to admit that she was more than a little nervous as she walked into her first class. She was also a little late. Principal Hadley had kept her too long as he gave her a pep talk before she started her first assignment as a high school history teacher.

One advantage that she saw from being late was that the class bell had already rung by the time she reached the classroom. All of the students were inside the room and most had selected a seat. Some were still standing as she entered, but they sat down while she dropped her books on her desk.

She wrote her name on the board, turned to the class, and took a deep breath before saying, "All stand for the Pledge of Allegiance."

Hadley had told her that this ritual was useful in getting the kids' minds focused on the fact that they were now in school and that the class had started, like the announcement that 'all stand' before a judge entered the courtroom.

She paused when she noticed that one boy, near the back of the room, remained slouched down in his chair.

"Excuse me," Shelby said, looking at the student. She stepped up between the rows to get closer to the student and make it clear who she was talking to. "Excuse me. What is your name?"

"Shawn," the student answered. He scarcely looked up, but remained focused on the pen that he fiddled with.

"Shawn. I would understand if you do not want to say the Pledge of Allegiance. However, I would like it if you would at least stand while the rest of the class said it, just to show a little respect to the flag."

The boy sat silently for a second, then shook his head and said, "I don't think I can do that, Ms. Johnson."

Shelby got a sudden knot in her stomach. The rest of the students were standing and ready to start. She knew that they were all evaluating their new teacher, wondering what they were in for. She had heard stories of classes that would take a young and inexperienced teacher, chew her up, and spit her out again.

She asked Shawn, "Why not?"

Shawn kept his eyes focused on his pen and remained slumped in his chair as if he was about to slide underneath his desk. When he spoke, his voice was soft, making it hard for Shelby to hear him. "Ms. Johnson, the words 'with liberty and justice for all' were put into the pledge as a way of showing contempt for anybody who would support tyranny and injustice, right? I mean, what we pledge to do when we say the Pledge of Allegiance is to promote liberty and justice and to stand up against tyranny and injustice. Patriots oppose tyranny and injustice. That's what the pledge tells us, right?"

Shelby shrugged. This was, after all, supposed to be an Amerycan History class, and they would be talking about these things soon enough. "Yes, of course. This country was founded on the idea that freedom is better than tyranny and justice is better than injustice. Good Amerycans care about these things."

Shawn glanced up and made eye contact with her only for a second. She noted that he had nothing on his desk but his history book. Otherwise, she would have thought that he was reading something that somebody else had made him say. Shawn continued, "And the part about this country being indivisible. That was because of the Civil War. The guy who invented the Pledge wanted us to swear that we would support the Union against rebels as a way of avoiding another bloody civil war. That's why he put the word 'indivisible' in the Pledge."

"Of course," said Shelby. "That's very good. I think it is a good idea that we all know what the Pledge of Allegiance means. That's why you should show respect for the Flag. These are all good things that you should be proud of and that you should want to defend."

"Okay," said Shawn. "Then, fifty years ago, Congress added the word 'white' to the Pledge of Allegiance. Now it says, 'one white nation, indivisible, with liberty and justice for all.' Doesn't this mean that, when we pledge allegiance to the flag, we are not only supposed to favor liberty, justice, and union, but also those who are white? Doesn't this say that anybody who does not support a white nation is unpatriotic – that he is as un-Amerycan as anybody who supports rebellion, tyranny, or injustice?"

"No," Shelby said with a sigh of relief. "No, not at all. Congress added the word 'white' to honor our heritage. It simply pays respect to the fact that all of our founding fathers were white, and that they clearly wanted to establish a white nation, and the fact that all of our past Presidents have been white."

"And all future Presidents should be white," Shawn added.

Shelby's smile vanished.

Shawn continued. "That's the real reason why Congress put the word 'white' in the Pledge of Allegiance, isn't it? They put it in when a bunch of white people were worried about the possibility of black people getting elected into public office in the 1950s, so they put 'white' in the pledge to tell people not to vote for black candidates."

"No," said Shelby hesitantly. "Our Constitution says that anybody can grow up to be President. That is another one of the things that makes this country great. We'll be reading about that, too."

"Ms. Johnson, name one black person in public office today."

Shelby hesitated.

"Ms. Johnson, imagine what would happen if I said I was running for public office. There would be whole throngs of white people out there saying that this is a white nation like it says in the Pledge, and calling this a white nation means we shouldn't elect black candidates. We are supposed to be voting against black candidates the same way we are supposed to be voting against candidates who support rebellion, or candidates who support tyranny, or candidates who support injustice. The Pledge says that voters should not support any of these types of candidates. Do you mean to tell me that Congress did not add the word 'white' to the Pledge of Allegiance fifty years ago as a way of putting anybody who was not white at a political disadvantage?"

"No, Shawn, I do not."

"Ms. Johnson, if you have been watching the news at all you know that one of our Presidential candidates – one of our white Presidential candidates – is being slammed by the mere rumor that he has refused to say the Pledge of Allegiance, a rumor that is not even true. In Colorado they held a special election to recall a city councilman who would not pledge allegiance to a white nation. Is there any sense at all to the claim that the Pledge is not used to make sure that we only elect white leaders who support a white nation?"

"Now, Shawn, you obviously know that you don't have to say the Pledge if you don't want to. I'm not asking you to say it. I'm just asking you to stand to show some respect for the good things that this country stands for. A lot of people died to buy you the freedoms you enjoy. Don't you think you owe them a little bit of gratitude?"

The boy bit his lip, and Shelby knew that she had struck a nerve. Still, Shawn said, "I don't see how that makes any difference, Ms. Johnson. Just because I am not actually being asked to pledge allegiance to a white nation myself, does this mean that there is nothing wrong with having everybody else pledge allegiance to a white nation? How does that make pledging allegiance to a white nation okay?"

Shelby said, "This is a free country. You should show your respect for all the good things this country stands for. You should be proud of our freedom and show some measure of gratitude to all of those soldiers and citizens that made this a free country."

Shawn looked up again, this time a little longer. "Ms. Johnson, if somebody was about to lead a room full of people in calling you . . . I'm sorry to say this, ma'am but I am just trying to illustrate a point here . . . if somebody were to stand before the whole school and insult you in some way by saying, for example, that you are a thief and a liar, and that he was asking everybody in the audience to shout, 'Shelby Johnson is a thief and a liar,' would the fact that he did not require you to say it mean that you should still stand and applaud the fact that it was said?"

A couple of the other children snickered and Shelby felt her face grow hot.

"Shawn," she said.

He continued to look at the pen in his hand.

"Shawn! Look at me while I am talking to you."

Shawn showed no signs of moving for a few seconds. Then he let out a long sigh. He put his pen down and sat up straight in his desk. Folding his hands in front of him, he turned toward her and held her gaze. He did not flinch or look away.

That did not help, Shelby thought to herself.

From the other side of the classroom, one of the students shouted, "You people will not be happy until you have removed all mention of the white race from the public square. White people built this country."

Shawn shrugged and answered softly, "At least I am not trying to remove all signs of white *people* from public office, which is what the Pledge was built to do to black people. This Pledge was designed to keep black people out of public office – to keep them out of the public square, except as spectators. I want the public square to be color blind. I see no problem with that."

"It's a problem if you're white!"

"That's enough!" Shelby shouted. "I have not given anybody else permission to talk!"

Just then, one of the other students – a white girl – sat down.

Shelby turned to her and said, "Jenny, I did not give anybody permission to sit down, either."

The girl remained seated. "It makes sense, Ms. Johnson. If the rest of the Pledge says that we're supposed to be against rebellion, tyranny, and injustice like he says, then doesn't 'white nation' mean we are supposed to be against black people? That's not fair."

"Jenny, stand up. What do you want me to tell your parents when they ask me about how things are going at school?"

Jenny looked over at Shawn, then back at Shelby. "Tell them that I stood up for a friend. They'll understand. And if they don't; well, it's no big deal to do the right thing when it's easy. A person really only shows her character by doing the right thing when it's hard."

Shelby took a step back.

"I'm sorry, Ms. Johnson," Shawn said. "I know that this isn't what you wanted. I promise that I'm not here to cause any trouble. However, don't ask me to stand and show respect for the idea that this has to be one white nation. I just can't do that. To be honest, I don't think you should be doing that either, but I will leave that up to you. Honest, Ms. Johnson, I'll just sit here quietly until you're done."

"Alright," said Shelby. "I'll discuss this with Principal Hadley and I'll let him decide." She stepped back to the front of the class and said, "Okay, let's say the Pledge of Allegiance." She put her hand over her own heart, turned to the flag, and started the ritual. Behind her, the bulk of the class joined in.

When they got to the middle of the Pledge, some of the students shouted, "...one WHITE nation..." as loud as they could.

Shawn did not flinch. They were doing just what the all-white Senate had done a couple of years earlier when a challenge to the Pledge made its way through the courts. He remembered watching the news clips of 99 Senators standing on the Capital steps saying the pledge, shouting 'white nation' as if to give special emphasis to the idea that non-whites had no place in Ameryca.

However, Shelby had not expected the outburst. She turned back toward the students and easily identified those who had shouted by their satisfied grins.

After they finished, the students took their seats, whispering among themselves and looking back at Shawn and Jenny. Shelby spoke hesitantly to the class. "Okay, let's start with introductions."

2. A Perspective on Scouting

When the bell rang at the end of the class, Shawn waited for the other students to leave. He stayed in his seat, securely holding onto his book and putting his foot through the strap on his backpack as it sat on the floor, while the other students filed past. At his previous school he had learned valuable lessons against making himself vulnerable to the "accidents" that angry classmates might have.

He was not the last to leave, however. Jenny, the white girl who had also sat through the Pledge of Allegiance, stayed back as well and approached him as the class emptied. "I have to say that, if you want to make friends on your first day of school, that was probably not the most efficient way to go about it."

"I can say the same to you," Shawn answered, while he put his book in his pack. "You didn't have to join me. Honestly, what you did, as a white girl, took more courage than I showed today."

"Thank you," Jenny said with a smile.

Shawn walked out of the room with Jenny beside him, making him nervous on a number of different levels.

"What's your next class?" Jenny asked.

"Chemistry," he answered. "However, I'm not going there. I've got something to do at the Principal's Office." He had stopped by a school bulletin board and stared at an announcement with the words Join the Youth Scouts written in large letters across the top. With the hallways starting to empty, he reached up and gave the paper a gentle tug, pulling it down.

"I don't think you should be tearing down other people's signs," Jenny said.

"I just want to show the Principal what I'm talking about."

"You're a trouble maker," said Jenny, smiling. "I'll come with you."

"You shouldn't do that," Shawn responded instantly. "You don't need to get into any trouble. Besides, what would your father say?"

Jenny smiled. "I told you in class what I think about what my father will say."

"I don't want you to come with me," said Shawn.

"Sorry. It's a free country."

Shawn had to hurry if he was going to make it to the Administrative Center before hall monitors started taking names, so he had no time to argue. He hurried down the hall, with Jenny close behind.

He had no appointment to see the Principal, who was busy getting the school organized on its first day. The secretary took his name and Jenny's, gave them permission slips good until the end of the period, and emailed excused absences to their teachers.

While Shawn waited, having Jenny there added significantly to his anxiety. He had rehearsed this encounter with the Principal a thousand times in his head, and not once did he imagine anybody with him.

Finally, Principal Hadley had a few minutes to spare. He got their names from his secretary and then called them into his office. He had a large office with a big oak desk, but he directed Shawn and Jenny to sit at a small round table near the window. After closing the door, he took a seat at the table and said, "Shawn, Jenny, what can I do to help you?"

Shawn found himself too nervous to speak, so he simply slid the announcement he had taken from the bulletin board across the table for Principal Hadley to read.

"I see," said Hadley. He picked up the paper, looked up at Shawn, and stood up from the table. "Okay, Shawn, I know that you're not thinking about joining since black people are not allowed in the Youth Scouts. Should I assume that you are opposed to this group recruiting on school grounds?"

"Yes, sir," said Shawn.

"Shawn, you should know that this school has a strict policy against discrimination. I can't kick a group off the campus simply because you don't like them here. If white kids want to get together and form a whites-only club where they can enjoy the company of other white kids, I don't think that I should be discriminating against them by trying to stop them."

Shawn took a deep breath. "Actually, Mr. Hadley, the fact that this is a bunch of white people who want to do things with other white people isn't the issue. The issue is that this club pushes the view that white people are morally superior to black people. Their official handbook says, quote, 'no person can grow into the best kind of citizen without the qualities inherent in the white race.' I have to live my life in the shadow of their prejudice. I have to live my life with school teachers, classmates, co-workers, and neighbors, many of whom have been told by this organization over and over again since they were young children that I, because I am a black person, am somebody to be feared because I lack some fundamental characteristic needed for morality."

"Well, I'm sorry, Shawn, but I can't stop them even if I wanted to. The federal government just passed a law saying that the Youth Scouts performs an important national service instilling important values in children and that no institution that gets federal funds – and we get federal funds – can deny access to the Youth Scouts. They are considered a fine and morally upstanding youth organization that gives children important values and life skills. It's the law; we can't discriminate." He put the sign back down on the table and slid it back in front of Shawn.

"They teach children important values," Shawn repeated. "Like, it teaches them to value the qualities of the white race over the qualities of those who are not white. Furthermore, even though the Constitution prohibits the government from supporting one race over another, the Government insists on supporting organizations that say that one race is morally superior to the other."

"They teach patriotism," Hadley said. "They teach a scout to be trustworthy, loyal, helpful, friendly, and a number of other values."

"In addition to the value that white people are inherently good and black people are inherently not so good," said Shawn.

"You might not like what they say, Shawn, but the school has no right to discriminate against somebody because we don't like what they say. We do have certain rights and freedoms in this country, and a person has a right to believe whatever they want to believe. Discriminating against people on the basis of their beliefs is wrong."

"Okay," said Shawn. "Let me see if I understand. An all-white Senate and an all-white House of Representatives pass a bill that then gets signed by a white President. This bill tells you that you have to let an all-white organization onto this school to tell the students that only white people are morally fit to become Senators and Representatives and Presidents. And the reason why these white politicians passed this bill is because discrimination is wrong."

"Yes, exactly," Principal Hadley said with a smile. "We recognize that discrimination is wrong, and we are not going to discriminate against groups like the Youth Scouts in this school. They are a good group. They teach a lot of important skills and values that it would be good for kids like you to learn."

"Kids like me," Shawn echoed.

Principal Hadley stammered, "Well, not kids like you, I mean . . . well, a lot of famous people were Scouts, and a lot of them will tell you that their scouting experience helped train them to become leaders in society."

"Famous people," said Shawn.

"Yes. People such as . . ."

"Famous white people," Shawn interrupted. He stood, then put his palm down on the announcement he had brought. As he closed his fist, he crumpled the paper within it. "I guess that kids who are not white either do not need these character-building experiences. Or maybe we just don't deserve them. Or maybe it is just a waste of time to try to teach black kids values like honesty, kindness, and loyalty."

"I will look into the issue a little further. I'll let you know what I find out," Hadley said. He turned toward Jenny and asked, "What is your interest in this?"

Jenny started to answer, but Shawn interrupted. "She is not a part of this. She was just curious, so I said she could come along if she wanted."

Professor Hadley said cautiously, "Good, then, is there anything else that I can help you with?"

"No, thank you, sir," said Shawn. "Thank you for your time." He and Jenny stepped around Hadley and headed out of the Administrative Center.

Principal Hadley watched them until they were a safe distance down the hall. He then told his secretary, "I would like to see their files. Also, find out who their teachers are. Warn them that these two might be trouble. If they become a problem, I want to nip it in the bud."

"Oh, not Jenny," said the secretary. "She has always been such a proper white child."

"Well, she is obviously falling in with the wrong crowd," Hadley answered. "There is a reason why we didn't let people like Shawn into the Youth Scouts. They're a bad influence. Maybe we can find a way to get Jenny away from him before he has more of a bad influence on her."

Shawn's information was up on Hadley's computer by the time he got back to his desk.

3. Patriotism

As the school day wore on, Shawn started to see some of the students that he passed in the halls staring at him, then whispering to their classmates. There were those who tried to bump him in the halls, knock his books to the floor, or trip him. However, he was well aware of all of those tricks and managed to walk the gauntlet without any serious missteps. The other black students, when they saw him, would look away nervously. A few of them whispered encouragement, but only when nobody else was listening.

During his study hall, the teacher handed him a note from Ms. Johnson asking him to meet her in her classroom at the end of the day. By the time the school day ended, the note was so badly worn that it felt more like cloth than paper, and was stained from the sweat from his palms.

When he entered Ms. Johnson's classroom she was alone at her desk. "Close the door," she told him. After he did so, she told him to pull one of the classroom seats up to her desk.

"I talked with Principal Hadley," she said. "He knew who you were."

Shawn braced himself for the results of that conversation.

Shelby continued. "Principal Hadley says that state law requires that we devote the first part of the class period to the Pledge of Allegiance. We don't have a choice in the matter. He also said that he did not see what your problem was. It's not like we're forcing you to pledge allegiance to a white nation. We're only asking you to stand and show respect while the rest of us pledge allegiance to a white nation. Still, he said that the law actually does not allow us to require that you stand. The way he said it, 'If he doesn't think that the country deserves even the least amount of respect from him, then he doesn't have to show it any.' And I think he has a point. We have abolished slavery. It is illegal everywhere for people to discriminate against you on the basis of your race."

"Kind of," said Shawn.

Shelby looked at him quizzically.

"Look up your state constitutions, Ms. Johnson. The Texas Constitution says that a person can be excluded from public office if he is not white. Arkansas, Maryland, Massachusetts, North Carolina, South Carolina, Tennessee, all have provisions in their state Constitutions that say that a person must be white to hold public office."

"It does not matter what the state constitutions say. The United States Constitution does not allow the states to have a racial test for public office. This nullifies the state constitutions."

"That's true. However, the states keep these provisions in their Constitutions," Shawn answered. "They keep these provisions as a way of saying that even though the federal government does not allow racial tests, the official State position is that only white people are qualified to hold those positions. Only white people would be allowed to hold these positions if not for the pesky interference of the federal government. A fair and just people would have seen the mere existence of a provision barring black people from holding public office as an embarrassment and removed them. But, I forgot. We are not a fair and just nation. We are a white nation. There's a difference."

"I don't think that you're being entirely fair, Shawn," Shelby said. "And I don't see what this has to do with the Pledge."

Shawn, however, continued speaking through Shelby's interruption. "Plus, the government continues to fund race-based organizations like the Youth Scouts that not only bar people like me from being members or employees, but organizations that openly declare that they do so because they hold us to be morally inferior. The government gives money to people to teach children that black people are morally inferior and do so while saying that these organizations promote important Amerycan values."

"Now, Shawn . . . "

"Ms. Johnson, you were saying that I shouldn't be upset that we pledge allegiance to a white nation since black people don't have it so bad here. But, Ms. Johnson, 'here' is still a place where the government has adopted a motto and a pledge that both say to white people, 'You are welcome here.' At the same time it says to blacks, 'You will merely be tolerated, because we think that you are not as good as the rest of us.' Tell me, Ms. Johnson, if the government values the loyalty of its black citizens, why does it not have a pledge that a black citizen can proudly give?"

Shelby simply shrugged.

"The Pledge of Allegiance says that good Amerycans support a nation that is indivisible, free, and just and that values its white citizens above all others. You are teaching them that those who do not support these goals are not good Amerycans. Saying that in a public school classroom – saying that to my fellow students – having the government teach people who I will have to deal with every day of my life that I am not a good Amerycan – is wrong. It doesn't matter that I don't have to repeat it. It is still wrong."

"I understand what you're saying, Shawn. Please realize, however, that saying the Pledge of Allegiance in the morning has nothing to do with race. It has to do with patriotism. It has to do with loving your country."

"It has to do with loving your country as long as it is white country, and with thinking that your country is not worth loving if it is not white. This is true in the same way that the Pledge tells us to love our nation as long as it is united, and to hate anybody who would try to rebel and divide the country. It is true in the same way that the Pledge tells us to love the nation as a nation with liberty and justice for all, and to hate anybody who would try to create tyranny and injustice. It's not a blank, empty, lesson in patriotism, Ms. Johnson. It is a claim that patriotism requires supporting an indivisible, free, just, and *white* nation. What else can it possibly mean, Ms. Johnson, to say that pledging allegiance to a white nation is a patriotic exercise?"

Shawn paused for a moment and took a deep breath. "Ms. Johnson, when you say that patriotism requires supporting a white nation you insult a lot of very patriotic Amerycans. There are a lot of black people who have risked their lives defending liberty and justice for all in this country. There were a lot of black people who fought in the Civil War to preserve the Union. When you say that patriotism means supporting a white nation, you're insulting my dad, Ms. Johnson. He died in Afghanistan two years ago. He was fighting for liberty and justice for all, Ms. Johnson. He certainly wasn't fighting for a white nation. So, Ms. Johnson, you do not realize just how wrong you are when you say that I am not honoring the people who served this country."

Shelby's eyes widened and her expression grew suddenly soft. "Really? I'm so sorry, Shawn."

"He was actually killed by friendly fire in a firefight near the Pakistan border. In the middle of a fire fight, somebody mistook him for the enemy – pretty much like the government does in sanctioning this Pledge. He certainly wasn't fighting for a white nation when he died. Does that mean that my dad wasn't a patriot? Doesn't it make sense that somebody who does not support a white nation can still have allegiance to Ameryca?"

"I suppose he could."

"Then why are you teaching your students that patriotism means supporting a white nation? And why are you telling them that my dad and thousands upon thousands of people like him who have fought and died – or even those who fought and lived – but who did not fight for a white nation - can't be patriots?"

"That's not what I'm saying."

"That's exactly what you're saying, Ms. Johnson. When you call pledging allegiance to a white nation a patriotic exercise, you are saying that those who do not favor a white nation are not patriots. It's the same thing as when you say that pledging allegiance to a nation with liberty and justice for all is a patriotic exercise. You're saying that patriots support liberty and justice for all, and those who do not support liberty and justice are not patriots. It's the same thing. How can you sit there and deny that?"

"Look, Shawn, I'm not going to debate you on this. I can understand where you're coming from, Shawn. I just think you're wrong, that's all. But, I understand. I can see how you can be upset. After all, you can't help the fact that you're not white. It's not like you could . . ."

Shawn slammed his palm down on his desk and stood up. He then saw that he had startled the teacher, so he apologized and returned to his chair. Forcing himself to calm down, he said, "That's not the point, Ms. Johnson. What if I could change my race? What if gene therapy made it possible for me to choose to be just as white as you are? You're still saying that a patriot would have to choose to be white because patriots support a white nation. You're still saying that the official government position is that citizens who choose to be black and do not agree to the superiority of a white nation are not patriotic Amerycans. Even if I could choose, what sense does it make to say that if I choose to remain black then I am not being patriotic?"

"This is going nowhere," Shelby said, still visibly shaken. "If you want, then you can leave the room when we say the Pledge of Allegiance. You obviously don't understand it and it seems like you're not in much of a mood to listen anyway. You've made up your mind. Now, you don't have to participate in the Pledge if you don't want to show respect to the flag. You don't have to listen. You don't even have to be present."

"That's very symbolic, Ms Johnson," Shawn answered. "As if pledging allegiance to a white nation is not insult enough to those who are not white, you drive the point home even further by having the black students leave the room. It's a lot like saying that this is a white nation, and black people should simply leave the country. I'm certain that the white students pledging allegiance to a white nation will be very comfortable doing so after the blacks have left and they are among their own kind. That's what the advocates of white power really want, isn't it, Ms. Johnson? They want the black people to leave."

"Stay, then," Shelby said tensely. "Stay in your desk and be quiet until we're done, just like you did today."

"That's also good symbolism, Ms. Johnson," Shawn answered. "After all, the true patriots – those who pledge allegiance to one white nation – are the ones who should do all the talking. If you are not willing to support a white nation, you should sit down and shut up. We should never think about including those who do not support a white nation. You'll be giving your students a very valuable civics lesson when you do this, Ms. Johnson, that there are two groups of people. There are the patriotic devotees to a white nation who have a voice in this country, and those who do not support a white nation whose only option is to sit down and shut up."

"Then what do you suggest, Shawn? Help me out, here. I'm running out of ideas."

"I suggest that you don't say the Pledge, Ms Johnson. Tell Principal Hadley that your job as a teacher does not involve telling your students that patriots are people who support a white nation, and that people who do not support a white nation are not patriots. Tell him that it's not your job to teach your students to be bigots or to denigrate Amerycans who fought for liberty and justice but not for a white nation."

"I can't do that. We have rules Shawn. We can't go breaking the rules just because we want to."

"Well, Ms. Johnson, I think one of your students said something real important today. Remember what Jenny said? Anybody can do the right thing when it is easy. You only see a person's moral character when she is willing to do the right thing when it is hard."

Shawn then stood slowly. "I promise, Ms. Johnson, I won't do anything to disrupt the class. I know how hard your job is. I really don't want to make it any harder. I'm just not going to support the idea that if somebody isn't white, then he can't be patriotic – particularly not after what happened to my dad. I couldn't do that, and you shouldn't expect me to."

"Fine," said Shelby.

"Good night, Ms. Johnson."

4. Conflicting Duties

All I want to do is teach, Shelby Johnson told herself while she watched the students file into her first period class. She was watching for Shawn to enter, hoping that he might decide not to come to school today.

It was a futile hope. She felt herself tense up the instant she saw him at the doorway. He came through the door, almost bumping into another student. He stepped back to give the classmate room to enter, then entered himself, taking a seat near the door.

He looked up at her, then closed his eyes and laid his head down on his desk.

The sound of the bell announcing the start of the class startled Shelby. She put herself on auto pilot. "All stand for the Pledge of Allegiance."

Shawn, of course, did not stand. He kept his head on his desk as if he was asleep.

Jenny remained seated as well, glancing at Shawn.

The boy sitting in the row next to Jenny leaned over and whispered something to her. Jenny's expression showed her anger, but she did not respond.

As the rules required, Shelby led the class in the Pledge. Again, she was startled when the class shouted, "one WHITE nation." That wasn't helping, and she resolved that she would put her foot down against that provocation.

When the Pledge ended and the students started taking their seats, Shawn suddenly stood. Standing at attention, his hand on his heart, and in a loud and clear voice he started, "I pledge allegiance to the flag of the United States of Ameryca . . ."

"No! Shawn, stop that!" Shelby shouted immediately.

He ignored her and continued. ". . . and to the republic for which it stands . . ."

Her mind raced to consider her options. Should she let him finish? What message would it give to the students for her to say that a black student cannot give his own Pledge of Allegiance?"

". . . one BLACK nation, indivisible . . ."

"That's enough!" Shelby shouted. Others in the class erupted in anger as well. One of the larger white boys flew out of his desk and charged towards Shawn, but was caught by a couple of other students and held back.

". . . with liberty and justice for all."

Shelby shouted, "Shawn, get out! Get out of my classroom! I will see you at the Principal's office. Take your stuff and get out, now!"

Others in the class started to heckle Shawn while he picked up his bag.

"Shut up!" Shelby said. "The next person to make a sound will get detention."

The class remained silent while Shawn approached the back door. As he left, Shawn turned to Shelby and said, "I am very sorry that I couldn't keep my promise." Then he left.

After Shawn had closed the door behind him, Shelby addressed the rest of the class. "Anybody who shouts 'white nation' while saying the Pledge ever again will get detention. That's a deliberate act of provocation and I will not stand for it in my classroom."

One of the students spoke up. "But that's what the Senate did, Ms. Johnson. When the Court of Appeals said that the Pledge was unconstitutional, they all went onto the steps of the capital and said the Pledge, and they shouted, 'one WHITE nation'."

"When you get yourself elected to the Senate, then you too can act like an ass. Not in my classroom. Now, I have to go to the Principal's office. Jim, go across the hall and ask Ms. Benson to keep an eye on my class. All of you will remain silent. You will read the first chapter in your books while I am gone."

As she started to leave, Shelby noticed the student next to Jenny take another anticipatory glance in her direction with a malicious smile. It seemed a poor idea to leave her here alone in a hostile classroom. "Jenny, come with me."

As Jenny stood to follow the teacher, several in the class taunted her. They seemed content with believing that she was also in trouble.

When Shelby got to the Administrative Center, Shawn was standing before the reception desk, and Principal Hadley was just coming out of his office. "What's going on here?" Hadley asked. He recognized Shawn and asked further, "What type of trouble have you caused now?"

After telling Jenny to sit down, Shelby approached the Principal, "We're still having a bit of a misunderstanding regarding the Pledge. I just need to talk to Shawn for a bit."

"What kind of misunderstanding?" Hadley asked.

"I think I can take care of it, Mr. Hadley," Shelby said.

Speaking slowly and deliberately, Hadley said, "I want to know what happened."

"It was nothing," said Shelby.

Mr. Hadley stared her down.

"Shawn remained seated during the Pledge, as did Jenny. But, when the Pledge was over, Shawn stood to give his own version of the Pledge. He pledged allegiance to 'one black nation' and that got . . . "

"Black nation?" Hadley asked, turning to Shawn with a look of contempt.

"I'm certain he was just trying to make a point."

"Ms. Johnson, come into my office," Hadley snapped.

Shawn watched as Shelby and Hadley entered the Principal's office; its large glass windows made it easy for him to watch them, and for them to watch him. He could not hear what they were saying, but he could see their mood in their body language. Mr. Hadley was dressing Ms. Johnson down and telling her to get in line, and Ms. Johnson was timidly and submissively trying to defend herself.

"Shawn," Jenny whispered, looking furtively around to see if anybody was paying attention.

"Shawn," Jenny repeated.

Shawn turned from the glass window into the Principal's office to face Jenny.

"Why did you say 'black nation'?" she asked.

"Because I wanted them to see how wrong it was to say 'white nation'. The way they felt when they heard me pledge allegiance to one black nation . . . well . . . that's the way I feel when I hear them pledge allegiance to one white nation. When a pledge like that excludes you it says that you're a lesser being, unworthy of a pledge that would include you. Besides, I also wanted them to see that the choice is not between saying 'white nation' or not saying it. I wanted them to see that the choice was between saying 'white nation' or 'black nation', and it's because both of them are wrong that the right thing to do is to say neither."

"Well, it didn't work," Jenny whispered. "Now everybody thinks you're some sort of militant who wants to wipe out white people."

"Militant? Was I carrying a weapon I didn't know about? All I did was pledge allegiance to the flag. If that's militant, than what is it when they pledge allegiance to the same flag? Why isn't that a militant act?"

At that moment the Principal's door opened and Hadley and Shelby stepped out. Hadley stepped up quickly and shouted to Shawn, "You stay away from her, young man. You have done enough damage as it is." He literally pulled Shawn away from Jenny and stood him up against the wall.

After walking out of the Principal's office, Shelby just kept walking out of the Administrative Center. She looked anxiously over her shoulder at Shawn, then turned towards her classroom.

Hadley continued. "Our classrooms are for learning, young man. Keep your political protests off of school property."

"Your students are learning to denigrate good men like my father," Shawn said. "He died for this country. He died because he thought a nation with liberty and justice for all was worth fighting for. He did not die – he would not die – for one white nation. You're trying to 'educate' me into believing that my dad could not be a patriot because he would not and could not pledge himself to 'one white nation'."

"Your dad has nothing to do with this," Hadley said. "Get this through your thick black skull. Nobody, I don't care what your race, has a right to disrupt the classes in this school."

"Why is it a disruption when I pledge allegiance to one black nation, but it is not a disruption when others pledge allegiance to a white nation? Why am I obligated to sit quietly and wait while they finish, but they are not obligated to sit quietly and wait until I finish?"

"Shawn, this country was founded by white men. If you paid attention in your history classes you would know this. This is a white nation. You would have us deny our heritage? If you don't like the law, take it up with your congressman. Do not come here and disrupt my classes."

"My white congressman?" Shawn asked. "I am supposed to politely ask my white congressman, representing a mostly white district all raised on a pledge of allegiance to white power to remove 'white' from the Pledge of Allegiance? When Al-Queida attacked us, what would you have thought of the idea of us going up to Bin Ladin and politely asking him – begging him – if he would kindly respect our right live in peace?"

"How dare you compare us to Al-Queida!"

"How dare you accuse me of comparing you to Al-Queida! When my dad went to Afghanistan he carried a gun. I come to school armed only with words. Why? Because I respect that *most people* will do the right thing once they learn what the right thing is. Only the most hate-filled bigots will insist that I do nothing while the school I attend spits on my dad's grave. My dad deserves better than that from the country he died to protect."

"I don't care what your cause is, you will not disrupt this school. You are confined to detention for the rest of the day; I'll have your teachers deliver your homework. If you insist on continuing this demonstration, you will be expelled, and where will that get you?"

Hadley turned around and told the school guard, "Take this boy to detention."

Hadley then saw Jenny, still sitting on the couch. "What are you here for?"

"I don't know," said Jenny. "Ms. Johnson asked me to follow her."

"Then follow her back to your class," Hadley commanded. He returned to his office, slamming his door behind him.

5. Outside Considerations

"You promised," Shelby Johnson said. She had come to the detention center under the pretext of bringing Shawn's homework to him. However, she really wanted to talk to him about the fact that he had broken his promise to her. "Last night, you looked me straight in the eye and promised that you would not disrupt my class. I actually thought you meant it."

"I did mean it," Shawn said. "But, later, I realized that what I promised to do was to sit quietly while you taught a class full of students that people like my dad do not deserve to be called patriots. I have an obligation to my dad, too. I have an obligation not to let the country he died to protect insult and degrade him, simply because he had no allegiance to a white nation. I either had to disappoint you, Ms. Johnson, or disrespect my dad. I'm sorry, you lost."

"It's not like that, Shawn. You're the only one who thinks that the Pledge of Allegiance disrespects those who don't favor a white nation. I talked to a lot of people about this, Shawn. Eighteen out of twenty people that I talked to were in favor of keeping the Pledge as it is now. They are in favor of 'white nation'. Even the two people who agreed with you said that the issue wasn't important – certainly not worth fighting for. They wanted to pick more important battles."

Shawn closed his eyes and took a deep breath before answering. "The fact that ninety percent of the people support pledging allegiance to white power in a school that is ninety percent white is not evidence that it's right. It's only evidence that the ninety percent of the people in this school who are white have no idea what justice really means. It's only evidence that ninety percent of the people have grown comfortable with injustice and the power that it gives them. They claim that white people have a special moral sense, yet what they really have is an ability to ignore the injustices they inflict on others and to use the fact that they do not 'sense' this injustice to say that there is none."

The detention room was built into the back of the library. It was originally built as a study room with a glass wall into the library and a door that students could close when they studied. It turned out to be a good place to keep students in detention where they could be confined and easily watched. This meant that the students in the library could see what was going on inside the study room and see who had detention.

Shelby lowered her voice to make sure that the students outside could not hear what was going on. "Fine, why can't you just let the white people have their pledge of allegiance to a white nation and get on with it? Why do you have to make such a fuss? To most people they're just words anyway. It's not as if they have much meaning."

"Then why did I get the reaction I did when I pledged allegiance to one black nation, Ms. Johnson? Some of the white kids in that class were ready to lynch me. Why is everybody else making such a fuss? The very fact that they are making so much noise is evidence enough that these are not just empty words. They have a purpose. The reason that white people get angry at the thought of removing these words is because they know that pledging allegiance to a white nation gives them power and takes power away from black people. They know that having young children do this every day until they are comfortable with it – is one of the most important tools they have for holding on to that power."

"People have been saying the Pledge for fifty years, Shawn. You're saying that you were the first person to figure out this secret meaning?"

"No, Ms. Johnson. You're not listening. I didn't figure out any secret meaning. Congress added 'white' to the pledge fifty years ago when they became afraid that some black people might actually get elected. They said so at the time they passed the law. Eisenhower himself said when he signed the law, 'From this day forward, millions of our schoolchildren will daily proclaim in every city and town, every village and rural schoolhouse, the dedication of our nation and our people to white power.' It's not a secret, Ms. Johnson. It's just that a lot of people have decided that if they speak the truth out loud that too many people will see how wrong it is. It's like the doctrine of 'separate but equal' before the 1950s, Ms. Johnson. No sane person could look at black schools and white schools before the 1950s and honestly say that they were separate but equal. However, as long as white lawyers did not admit this inequality out loud, white judges were willing to defend the system on the basis of this clearly obvious lie of 'separate but equal'."

"Shawn, they're not going to let you back into class unless you promise to behave yourself. They're just not going to permit it. I don't care what you say."

"Ms. Johnson, just don't tell the class that being a patriot means pledging allegiance to white power. Don't expect me to sit there while you tell everybody that people like my dad who did not support white power are as unpatriotic as anybody who would support rebellion, tyranny, and injustice for all. You're talking about my dad, Ms. Johnson."

"It's the law, Shawn."

"Yes. The law passed by white law makers telling you to teach other people's kids that they're not good Amerycans unless they pledge to continue to vote white people into office and to look down on anybody who does not agree that white people have a privileged place in this country."

"Don't do this, Shawn."

"It's your call, Ms. Johnson."

Shelby left Shawn's homework assignment on the table and left the room.

After Shelby left, Shawn settled down to do his school work. He had actually decided that detention was not a bad place to be. He was able to study quietly, and he actually did enjoy studying. Even when he was not doing school work, he was reading or studying the things that interested him; mostly history and science. He had read several chapters ahead in his Amerycan History text before the school guard arrived and said that Principal Hadley wanted to see him.

When Shawn arrived at the Administrative Center he saw his mother through the glass windows in the Principal's office. He stopped suddenly while his stomach fell through the floor. The secretary motioned for Shawn to go straight in. Hesitantly, he followed her instructions.

Principal Hadley saw Shawn through the windows and motioned him into the office. As Shawn entered, Hadley said, "I'll leave you two alone for a while." He turned to Shawn's mom and said, "Ms. Henry, I leave this matter in your capable hands," then left, closing the door behind him.

"Honey, this is a new school. You said you wouldn't get into trouble here."

"This is different, mom," Shawn said. "I'm not fighting. I'm not doing anything like that."

"They say that you're causing trouble in class, that you won't let the teacher do her job. What are you doing, son?"

"I listened to what you said, mom. I wasn't honoring dad by doing any of those things I was doing last year. Then, I started thinking about pledging allegiance to one white nation. That wasn't honoring dad either. Dad was more of a patriot than anybody here. None of them died for this country, but they tell everybody every day that those who don't support a white nation aren't patriots."

"You're father was a good man, Shawn. But I bet some of these people fought for their country, too. Just because they didn't die, that doesn't mean they didn't fight or that they wouldn't fight."

"Okay. Still, it's wrong, mom. It's wrong what they're doing."

"Maybe it is, son. But your dad wanted you to finish school. He wanted you to make something of yourself. He fought to give you a good life, son. Don't throw it away. You would break his heart."

"Mom, he fought to give me a good life by fighting those who would do us harm. That's what I'm doing, mom. Because the government is having everybody pledge allegiance to one white nation, people like dad – and people like me – can't do a lot of the things we would be good at doing. There was a poll recently where half of the people said that they would never vote for a black candidate because, after all, we are supposed to be a white nation. In the last election the President promised never to appoint any judges who would not uphold and defend white power, and people cheered. There is no more blatantly bigoted statement a person can make, and the people cheered. How many Presidential candidates this year have said that Americans want and should have white leaders? The students that have learned these lessons in contempt will become my neighbors, co-workers, and bosses when I grow up. Do you think that I will actually have the same opportunities I would have had if the government had not been getting them to pledge allegiance to the idea that white people are truly patriotic Amerycans and black people are not?"

The room fell into a long silence.

"Mom, I promise, it's like Gandhi. I've sworn that I'll never raise my hand in anger again. But that doesn't mean that I won't fight for what is right. If the school decides to punish me, I will take my punishment. If they quit saying that my dad wasn't a patriot, I'll quit protesting. If they keep saying that my dad wasn't a patriot, I'll speak my mind. But I won't hurt anybody, I promise. I'm standing up for what's right, mom. Just like dad did. And I probably won't even get shot at."

"Probably," Shawn's mother said, with a hint of a smile. "When you go back to detention, I want you to write down everything that happened. I want to know everything. We'll discuss it when you get home."

She picked up her gloves and her purse and headed for the door. Hadley saw her through the window and intercepted her.

"He's all yours, Principal Hadley," Ms. Henry said.

"Did you talk to him?" Hadley asked.

"We talked. We'll talk some more tonight," she answered. She said nothing else as she left.

6. Jenny

The next morning, well before the start of class, Shawn arrived at school and went straight to the Administrative Center. Ms. Johnson and Principal Hadley were there waiting for him. Hadley spoke formally and deliberately. "Shawn, before I can allow you to return to Ms. Johnson's class, I need you to apologize to Ms. Johnson about your behavior yesterday, admit that it was wrong, and promise never to do it again."

"I have to ask Ms. Johnson a question first," Shawn answered.

"What question?" Hadley asked.

Shawn turned to Shelby. "Are you going to be leading the class in the Pledge?"

"That's the law," Hadley answered for her. "You don't have to participate, but the state legislature requires that she begin first period with the Pledge of Allegiance."

Shelby answered with a shrug, gesturing towards Principal Hadley as if to say, "There's nothing I can do about it."

"If Ms. Johnson does not stand before the class and lead them in saying that my dad was not a patriot because he did not support white power, if she does not try to teach the class that patriotism requires supporting a white nation and those who do not support a white nation are not patriots, then I will have nothing to protest. If she stands before the class and denigrates people who do not support white power, then I will make my own pledge to black power instead."

"Fine. Back to detention," Hadley said. He summoned the school guard to escort Shawn back to the library. Once there, Shawn settled in, opened his math book, and got to work.

He was barely into the chapter when he was interrupted by the school guard opening the detention room door. He looked up and saw Jenny entering the room.

"I didn't know we were allowed visitors?" Shawn said.

"You aren't," the guard answered. "Jennifer is a guest."

"I seem to have gotten myself into a bit of trouble with the establishment," Jenny said with a mischievous smile.

"No talking," the guard announced. "That's the rule. You don't want to get into any more trouble than you already are. Jenny, you sit over here at this side of the table, away from Shawn. You're both to focus on your homework, nothing else. I will be watching the both of you."

Quietly, Jenny took a seat opposite the table from Shawn and got out her books. Through it all, a smile never left her eyes.

Shawn waited anxiously for the end of detention, which was at four thirty – well after the school day ended. He watched the second hand make its last lap around the clock, then asked Jenny, "What happened?"

"I waited until everybody else had said the Pledge of Allegiance, then I stood up and gave my version. I didn't say 'black nation.' I hope you don't mind. I just couldn't bring myself to say it. I just left out that part."

"What did Ms. Johnson say?"

"She didn't say anything. The rest of the class started to boo me, and she told them to sit down and be quiet. She let me finish. Then she sent me to the Principal's Office, and Mr. Hadley sent me here to detention."

"That's all?" Shawn asked.

"Well, Mr. Hadley gave me a lecture about you being a bad influence on me. He said how he hates to see me go down this path, and I have all of this potential and he would like to see me make better choices"

"Speak of the devil," Shawn said. Mr. Hadley had just entered the library with a middle-aged couple close behind.

Jenny gasped, "Those are my parents!"

Jenny's parents seemed quite well off. Her father was dressed in a well tailored suit and tie, and her mother was dressed as if she, too, had just left an executive board meeting with a laptop bag over her shoulder.

Mr. Hadley opened the door to the detention room and let the couple enter. Jenny's father spoke. "What is the meaning of this?" he asked.

"What I don't understand," Hadley said, "Is how a white girl from a perfectly good home could go along with this nonsense."

Jenny held her books close to her chest and said, "It's because I think that if we're supposed to live together in the same country we should treat each other with a little bit of respect. You can't put a white person up beside a black person and automatically say that the white person is the better person. There are a lot of really bad people in the world who happen to be white. So, maybe we shouldn't be looking at who is white and who isn't. Maybe we should be looking at what type of person they are. If they support liberty and justice, they don't have to be white."

Hadley answered, "I'm afraid that she thinks that she has got herself tied up in some noble cause. Kids are like that. They pick up some fanciful idea and before you know it they are crusading in the streets for free mocha for welfare recipients or something like that."

Jenny scowled at Principal Hadley, but Jenny's father answered, "We are talking about white values here. How can a black person have white values?"

"I don't know, dad, but sometimes black people do a better job of exhibiting white values than white people. That much is obvious. Besides, what are these 'white values'? You speak as if every white person is in agreement on every matter of right and wrong. I see white people argue all the time about what has value. So, why not say that black people can join in the debate? Sometimes they will agree with one group of white people. Sometimes they'll agree with another. Yet, I sincerely doubt that you will find any 'value' that really is actually a 'white value' – except the value that white people seem to put in having a white nation."

Ms. Bradford said, "A black person having white values. That doesn't even make sense, honey. They wouldn't even call it white values if that was the case."

"Maybe there's no such thing as white values, mom," said Jenny. "Maybe there are just values. Maybe white people aren't perfect and black people are aware of something that we just got wrong. We can argue about what is right and wrong and maybe we can learn something from each other. But, when the government tells us to pledge allegiance to a white nation, the government is taking sides."

Jenny's mother looked as if she was about to faint. "Jenny! No. You should never question white values. Our white values come from a moral sense that we got from a perfect God who would not have made any mistakes. We are incapable of error on these things. You should know that."

"Then why do white people disagree?"

"We'll discuss this when we get home, Jenny," Mr. Bradford said.

"This is the young man?" Jenny's mom asked, looking at Shawn.

"Yes, Ms. Bradford."

"Young man, I ask that you find better things to do with your time than to corrupt my daughter." She then held her hand out towards Jenny and added, "Come along, dear."

Jenny went with her mom, leaving her dad and Principal Hadley behind. Mr. Bradford waited until the women were out of earshot and added, "I realize that you people have difficulty determining right from wrong, so I will put this in terms that you can understand. If I catch you anywhere near my daughter, you will suffer the consequences, and that is a promise."

He did not wait around for Shawn's rebuttal. He spun on his heel and was out the door at a quick pace, catching up with the women.

"What am I going to do with you, Shawn?" Principal Hadley said. "I can't let this continue. You are a disruption to the school. Either you need to start living by our rules, or I will have no choice but to convene a hearing to have you expelled."

"Only those who accept the practice of pledging allegiance to white power are allowed to attend a public school," Shawn said.

"You have the option, according to state law, of sitting quietly during the Pledge of Allegiance."

"While everybody goes through this ceremony that says that patriotism means supporting white power."

"You have the option of saying the Pledge with the rest of the class, or of sitting quietly while the rest of the class says the Pledge of Allegiance. Those are your options. Tomorrow I will give you one last chance to take one of those two options. If you do not agree to the rules, I will convene a board of expulsion. I don't care how unfair you think it is. I don't care if you feel insulted. I don't care about anything but allowing my teachers to teach their classes without disruption. Tomorrow, you agree to live by the rules, or you will be expelled. Do you understand me?"

"And Jenny, will you expel her, too?"

"If I have to. Hopefully, with her parents' guidance, we can get through this phase she is going through without doing permanent harm to her future. She really does have a promising future ahead of her. Your future depends on how smart you are when you come to school tomorrow. Sleep on it, Shawn. Choose the right option."

7. Appeasers

With his detention for the day having been served, Shawn dropped his books into his backpack and headed down the nearly deserted halls of the school. There were more teachers than students around, and the students that remained did not seem to be paying him any attention.

He had just stepped off school grounds when he heard somebody call his name. He turned and saw three black students approaching. The one in the middle he recognized as Paul, who was the only other black student in his physical education class on the one day he actually attended class. He did not recognize either of the other two. However, they walked slightly behind him on his left and right like body guards.

"What do you want?" Shawn asked as they approached.

None of the three answered. They continued to walk towards him without a word. Shawn let his backpack drop from his shoulder and grabbed the strap in his hand.

Paul stepped right up to Shawn and shoved him, with both hands, back off of the sidewalk. As Shawn's arms went out to keep from falling, he dropped his backpack.

"What do you think you're doing?" Paul asked. "Everything was fine here until you come along. Now all the white students are looking at us as if we're all potential terrorists."

"What do you want me to do about it?"

"Quit getting everybody riled up with this 'black nation' nonsense. We have had peace at this school for years. They still lynch blacks in some parts of the world, you know. Why do you want to mess things up for us? For two days now all I've heard is how this militant black wants to do away with all of the whites."

"I'll give you a clue, Paul. The reason things are so cozy for you here is because you have all agreed to sit under the table begging for table scraps while the white people eat You're like a bunch of slaves serving a white master who only beats you when you act up. So, you've learned not to act up. You've learned not to cause any trouble. All you need to do is to pledge allegiance to white power like the white people want you to do. You know, there are other parts of the world where things are even cozier for blacks. Those are places where blacks have learned to stand up for themselves and quit whimpering every time the master raises his voice."

"Don't you ever call me a slave!" Paul said, shoving Shawn again.

The kid to Paul's left, a tall and slender kid, added, "Nobody at this school feels oppressed or brainwashed as a consequence of muttering the words 'white nation'. I don't."

"Listen to yourself," Shawn said. "You can stand there and say that a class full of white students pledging allegiance to a white nation doesn't make you feel oppressed and brainwashed. If that's the case, then the fact that you are not feeling oppressed is proof enough that you have been successfully brainwashed. Trust me, no just nation would tolerate people pledging allegiance to a white nation. Having black people pledge allegiance to a white nation is sick. It means that they have made you comfortable with the idea that the government views you as inferior to those who are white. It means that they have taught you your place in society as beneath them and you have made yourself happy there. I bet I can also find women in certain cultures today who claim that they do not feel oppressed being denied the right to vote, to an education, to decent medical care, to marry who they please, or to go out in public by themselves. They fact that they do not feel oppressed also merely proves that they, too, have been successfully brainwashed."

"Don't you get it?" Paul said. "We're not suffering here. You don't find black people tied to fence posts and left to die in this school district. There aren't gangs hunting for black people with the intent of beating them to the edge of their lives. Except for a stupid pledge and a few stupid signs, they leave us pretty much alone."

"They leave you alone, as long as you do not aspire to be anything important or to do anything important. That's what I said, the content slave probably gets left alone, too. It's the black person who demands equal treatment, and the woman who doesn't know her place, who risks the wrath of those who would be their masters."

"Except you're making it bad for all of us," said Paul.

The tall one spoke again. "If you're going to change things, you have to make alliances. You have to work with people. You have to compromise and build up a coalition. There aren't enough people willing to give up a pledge to a white nation to form any type of coalition. You've got to fight the battles you can win, and know when to walk away."

Right," said the other student who stood at Paul's left. "Haven't you ever heard that you can attract more flies with honey than with vinegar?"

"You call this honey?" Shawn asked, rubbing his chest. "Your honey has a really bitter aftertaste."

"You're not listening, man," Paul said, stepping up close. "You're just making them mad. You're not going to get anybody to change their mind by ridiculing and belittling them and making them mad."

"Do you expect that I can get them to change their mind by stroking their egos and telling them how wonderful they are? The first step in getting somebody to change their mind has to be telling them that the mind they have today is one that they need to change. The only way to get them to change their mind about a school ritual that denigrates blacks is by telling them that a school ritual that denigrates blacks is something that good people would change."

Shawn then faced the tall kid. "As for your alliances, you form your alliances if you want. That's not my job. If you want to tell them that I am some mean and vicious militant black person so that they will pat you on the head and say, 'good boy,' you go ahead and do that. Don't forget to wag your tail and to play dead when they ask you to. You might even get some extra table scraps if you made yourself sufficiently cute and adorable."

The tall kid clenched a fist for a second, but did not budge. "Pledge to black power, and they'll just see you as a threat. They'll see all of us as a threat."

"Actually," Shawn said. "All you're saying is that we're supposed to act like nice, peaceful little slaves in order to keep the master happy. That way, he won't beat us as badly. Maybe that's true. Maybe telling the master that slavery is evil is a good way to get beaten. But slavery is still evil. And slavery can't be made right by threatening to beat anybody who says otherwise."

"Leave it alone," Paul repeated. "If you were the only one to get beaten, I would tell you to go enjoy yourself. But you're not. All of us are going to suffer. You have no right to do that to us."

"Wrong, again," Shawn said. "That's like saying that the cop who dies trying to arrest a criminal is the fault of the judge who signed the warrant. That's wrong. The wrong being done here is being done by those who insist on a pledge of allegiance to white power. You need to remember that. You need to decide that you should be condemning the person who killed the cop, not the person who signed the arrest warrant. You need to decide if you are on the side of what is just and right, or if you're going to help those who support injustice because you happen to find it more convenient and more comfortable in the short run."

"You're still not listening. You're going to get a lot of innocent people hurt because the white people are not going to accept the idea of not pledging allegiance to white power and they will attack anybody who threatens that position."

"Let's find out," said Shawn.

"Let's not find out!" Paul said, again shoving Shawn. "We find out when people get hurt."

"You know, it's actually ironic," Shawn said. "It seems that we have fundamentally different views of what white people are like. You think that white people are hopelessly violent and unjust so that we can never expect anything better from them then some minimal level of abuse and denigration. I think that most white people are decent folks who will do the right thing once they figure out what the right thing is. Some of them will get angry and abusive. They will threaten and rant and lie and do whatever they can to keep their power. They will be in the majority at first. But, eventually, those who care for what is right will outnumber those who do not care about the injustices they inflict on others. Then things will change."

"Don't expect our help," Paul said. "A lot of us don't share your militant ways, and we're going to make sure that they know whose side we are on." He waved to his friends and they turned back up the street. Shawn picked up his backpack and continued on his way home.

8. Hating Ameryca

Principal Hadley had given Shawn the night to choose between submitting to a Pledge of Allegiance to a white nation without protest, or being expelled from school. Shawn did not need even a minute to consider his options. He imagined himself sitting in class while Ms. Johnson taught his classmates that patriotic Amerycans support a white nation, and he could not even imagine himself bearing the insult in silence. The only outcome he could imagine accepting was one in which Ms. Johnson refused to give her class this government mandated lesson in bigotry.

That evening, during supper, he broke the news to his mother that he would be expelled. "I'm doing this for dad," he told his mother. "I'm doing this because he was a patriot, even if he didn't have any allegiance to one white nation."

"I know your dad never approved of pledging allegiance to a white nation," she said to him in response. "He refused to say the Pledge of Allegiance in the military. Every time he re-enlisted he would simply cross out any reference to defend and protect a white nation and put in a reference to protect and defend the Constitution instead. The Constitution explicitly prohibits Congress from passing laws that favor one race over another. But you really do have to finish school, Shawn. You're not going to get anywhere if you don't finish school, and we can't afford private school."

"I can continue studying even if I'm not going to school," Shawn told his mother.

"Shawn, you know, a lot of people leave high school every year saying that they can study at home and still get a degree. However, it almost never works out. Once they're out of school, life gets in the way. Time just seems to slip by until they find themselves sitting in a cheap apartment with a wife and three kids on a winter night wondering how they're going to pay to replace the furnace."

"It'll be different with me, mom. I know how important it is to have an education."

"Every one of those other students said that it would be different with them, too. It just never turns out to be much different. I want you to stay in school, Shawn. I don't want to see you on the street."

"Mom, I'll get up at 6:30 like I always do. I'll study just like I do in school every day. If I get a job, it will be in the evening or on weekends. But, I have to do this, mom. I can't go back into that school and apologize and say I was wrong to insist that they not denigrate dad and everybody like him. I'm not wrong, and I am past the point where I can say that it doesn't matter."

Shawn's mother simply nodded her head in agreement.

"I'm not most kids, mom," Shawn said.

"I know. You're a lot like your dad, and he would be proud of you. When your father went off to war, I didn't want him to go. He had already been approved for a transfer when his unit got called up. He asked them to revoke his transfer so he could serve with his unit. He said he couldn't live with himself if he tried to get out of it because if everybody thought that way, nobody would ever do the dirty work. And none of us would ever be safe. I was scared, but I was also proud of him for agreeing to do the dirty work. Shawn, don't do anything stupid."

"I'll do it just like Gandhi did, mom. I won't raise a hand against anybody, no matter what they do to me. But I won't give in either."

The next day, when Shawn got to school, he found a group of students gathered around the front door. When they saw Shawn, they parted, leaving him a path to a sign that somebody had taped to the door. The sign showed a white kid standing before the flag, his hand over his heart, and a caption below the flag that said, "Why does Shawn Henry hate Ameryca?"

Shawn clawed the sign off of the door and looked around. He counted four teachers standing within line of sight of the door, yet none of them had thought to even ask what was going on. Crumpling the paper in his hand, he marched in the direction of the Administrative Center.

Jenny intercepted him. She handed him another version of the same sign. This one said, "Why do blacks hate Ameryca?"

"I can tell you why," Jenny said in a soft whisper as she matched Shawn's stride. "Because Ameryca is a white nation. If you hate the idea of this being a white nation, then you must hate Ameryca."

"If Ameryca is a country that pushes its loyal citizens to pledge allegiance to white power, then it deserves to be hated," Shawn grunted.

"Say that a little louder, Shawn," Jenny said. "Then you won't have to worry about detention any more, not until you're released from the hospital, if you live that long."

Shawn stopped. He found a chair sitting against the wall of the hallway and climbed on top. He shouted, "Ameryca is either a great nation that values liberty and justice for all. Or it is a bigoted nation that values white power. It's one or the other. Take your pick. It can never be both."

Two teachers were already working their way through the crowd to call him down, but Shawn did not give them time. He stepped down and continued toward the Administrative Center. "Sure, the teachers are not at all concerned about somebody posting a sign asking why blacks hate Ameryca, but let somebody question white power and they come running."

Side by side, Shawn and Jenny entered the Administrative Center, where Principal Hadley and Ms. Johnson stood waiting.

Principal Hadley greeted them with a smile. "Jenny, let's start with you. Show Shawn your good sense. I trust that your parents had a long and serious talk with you about the importance of staying in school."

"Yes, Mr. Hadley," Jenny said with a wide smile. "They taught me the importance of an education. They also taught me the importance of doing what's right. They are the ones who taught that a person does not show her moral character by doing the right thing when it is easy. She shows her moral character by doing the right thing when it is hard. I'll accept my punishment, but I will not support a Pledge of Allegiance to white power."

Hadley reached forward, took hold of Jenny's arm, and dragged her away. "Jenny, this isn't some noble cause. Shawn is just a troubled kid trying to get attention. It's the Pledge of Allegiance we're talking about here, not the abolition of slavery."

"It's a pledge to white power, Mr. Hadley. Of course, being white, I have nothing against white power. Even if white people are the best leaders, they are not the best leaders because they happen to be white. There are a lot of white people who are atrocious individuals. A person is a good leader because of intelligence and moral character. I know it is said that blacks lack the moral sense of white people – that God gave whites an infallible moral code that nobody else has. But, from what I see, Shawn's got a lot better moral sense than a lot of the white people around here. I sense that, and I'm white."

"Jenny!"

"There are a lot of private schools that my dad can get me into, Mr. Hadley. But you're going to have to expel me. In the mean time, I know my way to the detention hall." Jenny gave a polite bow, and headed towards the library.

"Look at what you've done," Hadley said to Shawn. "I suppose that expecting you to apologize and put an end to this is out of the question."

"I suppose that expecting you to apologize for denigrating my father as a non-patriot and teaching my classmates to look down on people who do not support white power is out of the question," said Shawn. He held up the sign that Jenny had given him. "I suppose that expecting you to put an end to this is out of the question as well."

Hadley sneered at the sign. "I talked to the students behind that. They said that the sign really means, 'Why do black people act like they hate Ameryca.'"

"Mr. Hadley, the question, 'Why is the sky blue?' means the same as 'The sky is blue. Why?' The question, 'Why do blacks hate Ameryca?' is the same as, 'Blacks hate Ameryca, Why?' Your decision to accept their lame explanation makes as little sense a math teacher accepting a student's claim that the number '5' she gave as an answer is really a '7', after being told that 5 is the wrong answer."

"Guard, get him out of my sight," Hadley said. He turned and went into his office while the school guard took Shawn to the detention center.

9. Reasons and Causes

"You have a visitor," the school guard said as he held the door open for an elderly lady.

The lady fumbled to move her books from one arm to the other to free up her hand, which she offered to Shawn. "I'm Ms. Miller. I'm the school psychologist," she said.

Shawn shook Ms. Miller's hand, nodded acknowledgement, but said nothing.

While Ms. Miller took a seat at the table, the guard commanded Jenny to pack up her books and escorted her to another table in the library.

"I asked Principal Hadley for a chance to come to speak to you," Miller said. She pulled a folder from her pile of papers and opened it. "I would really hate to see something happen here that all of us will have reason to regret."

She folded her arms across her open folder, looked at Shawn, and said, "I understand your father died two years ago."

"Yep," said Shawn.

"That must have been very hard on you," said Ms. Miller.

"It wasn't one of my better days."

"It also says here that you were a good student, until that happened. I went through your records from your previous school. Fighting. Disrupting class. Talking back to your teachers. You were suspended once for showing up drunk at school."

"That also wasn't one of my better days."

"I think I know what's going on here, Shawn. Losing a parent is a terrible thing. It makes you angry. It makes you want to strike out and hurt people, just like you've been hurt. All of this acting out is quite understandable, given your history. It's just that, I hope you understand, there are socially acceptable ways of dealing with one's grief. You're hurting yourself, and you're hurting the people around you."

"People around me? Like, who?"

"Like Jenny. Like your mother. Like Ms. Johnson. She cares about you, Shawn. She wants you to come back to her class."

Shawn smiled. "I get it. You think that my protest over the Pledge is because I am mentally unbalanced. No sane person could question pledging allegiance to a white nation. I don't like the idea that the school has a ritual where they encourage students to say that people like my parents aren't patriots because they didn't fight and die for white power, and that means I'm mentally ill."

"You are not mentally ill, Shawn," Ms. Miller said. "When we are in grief, we go through a well understood set of phases before we move on. The first thing we do is deny what we don't want to believe. When you were first told that your father had been killed, you probably didn't believe it. You probably thought it was a joke. Even after you were told, you were probably expecting him to call or to write or to come through the door. Only, it never happened."

"Ms. Miller, with all due respect I can easily imagine people in your profession 150 years ago, going out to the slave that is chained to the whipping post, and saying, 'Toby, this is the third time you've tried to escape. You keep insisting on this destructive behavior. Let me help you. Work with me, and I'll teach you how to accept slavery so that you can go on to live a full life, and you will never again face another whipping.'"

"You are not tied to a whipping post, Shawn."

"I'm in detention. They're going to try to expel me."

"You brought this upon yourself, Shawn. Do you really think that we can tolerate students disrupting class?"

"That's what I mean, Ms. Miller. I can hear you telling the slave on the whipping post, 'You brought this on yourself, Toby. Do you really think that the plantation master can tolerate allowing his slaves to run away?'"

"That's not fair, Shawn. I'm here to help," Ms. Miller said, her voice quivering with a hint of anger.

"Am I wrong?" Shawn asked.

"That's not important . . ."

"That's the only thing that's important. Ms. Miller. If I'm wrong, I'll apologize. If it's true that patriotism means pledging allegiance to white power, and that no person who refuses to pledge allegiance to a white nation can be a patriot, even if he dies protecting this country, then I will apologize. If it's not true, then I have nothing to apologize for. If I'm wrong, you can do your psycho analysis and try to find out how I became so delusional. If I'm right, then I'm right. It doesn't matter how I came to understand this truth. What matters is that I understand this truth."

"Shawn, I want you to listen to me. You are the only one who thinks that you are doing the right thing – you and Jenny Bradford. Jenny's at that rebellious stage where she wants to assert that she is her own woman, and not her father's daughter. She wants to show her father that she doesn't have to agree with him. If you're willing to work with me, we can set up some appointments to help you get through these issues about your father, and I think I can convince Principal Hadley to keep you in school. All you have to do is accept my help, obey the rules and work with me on finding a more positive way of expressing your grief."

"It doesn't matter how many people agree with me, Ms. Miller," Shawn said. "It matters whether they have reasons for agreeing with me that make sense. It doesn't matter how many people think the world is flat. If I think the world is round and I can give evidence for my belief, then that is what matters – not the number of people who think it is not true. Is it legitimate for a government to push teachers into teaching students that patriotic Amerycans support white power? Yes, a country full of white people might be more than happy to have the government push white power. But is it right?"

"Obviously, it is quite acceptable, Mr. Henry, because the people do, in fact, accept it. We have nearly two dozen black students in this school and even they are not rallying to your cause, Mr. Henry. Even they realize that a white nation has a right to select white rulers."

"We are not all white," said Shawn.

"But you are the minority, Shawn. This is a democracy. In a democracy, the majority rules. If the majority of the people are white, then they rule. If the majority thinks that it is a good idea to press kids into pledging allegiance to a white nation, then the issue is settled. The law is passed and it becomes the law of the land that we press children into pledging allegiance to white power. There is no other form of legitimacy than that, Mr. Henry. There is no better proof possible that something is acceptable than the fact that it is accepted. What is not acceptable is your disrupting class to say something that is manifestly untrue, that white rule for a white nation is not acceptable."

Shawn shook his head.

"Now, Shawn, I'm sorry about your father, but you need to make a place for yourself in the world now. Your father is gone. You are still here."

"I'm hearing that voice again, Ms. Miller. 'Toby, how can you say that it is not acceptable for white people to hold black people as slaves when, quite obviously, white people accept it. You're statement is manifestly untrue. Black slavery quite obviously is acceptable, as I can prove by the simple facts that you are black, Toby, and you are a slave."

"We are not talking about slavery, Shawn."

"I'm not talking about slavery," said Shawn. "I'm talking about the claims that people can make to defend things like slavery and pledging allegiance to a white nation that actually don't make any sense. The claim that you are making, Ms. Miller, that it is acceptable because people accept it, does not hold water. Slavery can still be wrong even if ninety percent of the letters sent to some state senator favor slavery – and even if we hear nothing from the slaves, perhaps because they have not been taught to write, or they have been made afraid to express their opinion."

"Shawn, I really would like to help you. Unfortunately, you have to take the first step. You have to admit that you need help dealing with the loss of your father, and that fighting and drinking and disrupting class are not acceptable ways of acting out."

"Ms. Miller, I am not fighting and I have not been accused of fighting. I am not drinking and I have not been accused of drinking. As far as your analysis goes, you are probably right about what I was going through last year. My mom showed me that I don't honor my father by turning into a violent drunk. My mom showed me that I don't honor my father by fighting except when I fight for what is right, like he did, and to never try to persuade people with violence. You're a year late, Ms. Miller. This year, I am not disrupting class because of some unresolved issues with my father. I am disrupting class because Ms. Johnson gets up in front of the class every morning and tells the class, 'All together now. Shawn Henry's father, and any like him who do not support a white nation, are not patriots.'"

"My door is always open, Shawn," Ms. Miller said as she collected her gear and stood up to leave. "Some people need to hit bottom before they start to claw their way up. Some people never make it back. I'm here to help, so, when you want help, please come see me. Even after you get expelled, if you call to make an appointment, I can see you and help determine if you are safe to come back."

She tried to shake hands again, but her shifting bundle of papers made that difficult. Shawn walked past her and held the door open for her.

"Good bye, Shawn."

10. Tolerance and Moral Superiority

"I'm here to explain what is going to happen tomorrow," said Vice Principal Lewis as he sat across the table from Shawn. "Normally, Principal Hadley would do this himself, but you have him pretty riled up."

"Of course I have him riled up," Shawn answered. "He's white, and he is in a position of power. He has a lot of white friends in positions of power. Naturally, he has an affection for policies and rituals that support white people in positions of power. One of those rituals is this national pledge of allegiance to a white nation. I am challenging that practice. So, naturally, he is upset."

"I'm not here to discuss the merits of the case, Shawn," Lewis said. "I'm simply here to explain the rules. Now, Principal Hadley has scheduled an expulsion hearing for tomorrow morning at 9:00 am. He has already talked to your parents . . . ."

Shawn interrupted, "Principal Hadley must have amazing powers if he talked to my father. He's dead."

"Whoever is responsible for raising you," Lewis said impatiently. "Your mom?"

Shawn nodded.

"She said that she will come for the hearing. In addition, you are allowed to have an advocate. An advocate is somebody from the school who knows our rules. This is an administrative hearing, not a court of law, so there is no place here for a lawyer. If you do not agree with the decision reached in this hearing you will, of course, have the option of hiring a lawyer and filing a complaint in civil court. That's where you'll get a lawyer, but not here. Not yet."

Lewis took a drink of water, then continued. "Like I said, you are allowed to have an advocate. Typically, we ask one of the guidance councilors to do this. They know the rules and are partially responsible for enforcing them. If you would like to speak to any of the guidance councilors I would be pleased to arrange for you to meet with them later on today. Would you like one of the guidance councilors to be your advocate tomorrow?"

"How do I know?" Shawn answered. "Guidance councilors are hired by the school. The school is paid for by government money. The government is run by white people who, for the most part, are quite infatuated with this idea of a pledge of allegiance to a white nation. It hardly makes sense to have somebody bought and paid for by the institution of white power representing me at this hearing."

Lewis answered with a shrug. "I can arrange for you to speak to Mr. Fox, if you would like. I don't need a decision right away, but time is short."

Shawn shrugged. "I guess it won't hurt. I'll talk to Mr. Fox."

Lewis scribbled a note onto his pad, then continued, "If the decision goes against you, then you will be escorted to your locker to pick up your things and you and your mom will be escorted off the campus. If you attempt to return to campus without an appointment, then you will be arrested for trespassing."

"How long does it take the committee to reach a decision?" Shawn asked.

"Typically, they make the decision on the same day – in less than an hour, actually."

"And if the decision goes in my favor?"

Lewis took off his glasses and rubbed his eyes. "If the board decides in your favor then you will be allowed to return to class. Now, I'm not on the board and nobody is asking me to be impartial. I can tell you honestly, Shawn, that this hearing is a mere formality. You will have a chance to make your case, but the Board will vote against you and you will be removed from the school system. The only thing that can save you is an apology and a promise not to disrupt class again. If you are prepared to do that, then we can get that over with now and avoid the hearing. Is that what you want to do?"

"Are you officially prepared to sit there and be quiet while the school you work for officially calls your wife a whore and a slut whose only interest is in her own pleasure?"

Lewis grew noticeably red, but did not answer.

"Well, then, I'm just as ill prepared to sit there while the school officially declares that my dad was not a patriot because he had no allegiance either to establishing or preserving a white nation."

"Then the Board will vote for your expulsion, Shawn," Lewis said. While he spoke, he slid a stapled set of pages across the table. "Those are the formal rules, in case you want to read them. Do you understand each of the rules as I have explained them to you?"

"I think so," said Shawn. "I would like to speak to Mr. Fox before I say so for sure."

"If you insist," Lewis said. "When you're satisfied, sign the form at the front of the document and I will pick it up at the end of the day. If you have any questions, tell the guard that you need to see me."

"Yes, sir," answered Shawn.

A few minutes after Vice Principal Lewis left, the guard returned to escort Shawn to see Mr. Fox. Shawn found Fox in his office, greedily downing a thick sandwich. "I hope you don't mind if I eat," said Fox through a mouth full of lettuce and bread. "The first days of school are murder. There's no free time."

"Not at all," said Shawn, sinking into a small couch on the other end of the office.

"Do you want me to represent you before the Council?" Fox asked slowly, almost nervously.

"That depends. What do you think of my case?"

Swallowing, Fox answered, "Okay, I will be completely honest with you, Shawn. I think that what you are trying to do goes against the very spirit of a free society. You're trying to impose a minority view on the majority. The majority of the people in this country are white. They have voted to approve a pledge of allegiance to a white nation. That's the majority decision. You come along with a very small minority view that we shouldn't be pledging allegiance to a white nation, and you're going to disrupt class until you get your way. It's a lot like a two-year old throwing a tantrum in the aisle at the supermarket unless he gets his lollipop."

Shawn found himself smiling as he listened to Mr. Fox. "So, Mr. Fox, imagine that you are a slave. Imagine that we live in a society where most of us are not slaves, but a minority of us are slaves, and you belong to that minority. You decide that you are going to protest the slave laws by refusing to work. Then, one of the work leaders comes to you and says, 'Mr. Fox, as I see it, your protest goes against the very spirit of democracy. The majority of the people, have decided to enslave a minority of the people. You have decided that you don't like that decision. So, like a two-year old screaming until he gets his lollipop, you decide that you are going to disrupt the work shift until the white slave masters give you what you want. You are going to protest until you have successfully imposed your minority position on the majority."

"Slaves are not allowed to vote," Fox said.

"What if they were allowed to vote? We are going to vote on slavery. Eighty-five percent of the people who will not be slaves vote in favor slavery, while the fifteen percent who become slaves vote against the proposal. You are on the list of people to become slaves. We have our majority and minority positions. Yours is a minority position. However, you're not willing to accept the majority position that says that you're supposed to be a slave. You reject it. So, now, you are going to throw a tantrum until the majority gives in and accepts a decision against slavery that only fifteen percent of the population actually agrees with."

"We're not talking about slavery, Shawn. We're talking about the Pledge of Allegiance."

"We're talking about pledging allegiance to white power."

"Which nobody is forcing you to do if you don't agree with it. See, we are about tolerance. We are against forcing our views on others. We are not going to make you pledge allegiance to white power if you do not want to. But you don't go along with that position. You think it's perfectly acceptable to force us not to pledge allegiance to white power. We give you the freedom to choose to pledge allegiance to white power or not. You do not want to give us any freedom. You want to ban a pledge of allegiance to white power."

"Actually, no, Mr. Fox." Shawn answered. "You can pledge allegiance to white power as often as you like. I'm not talking about a private endorsement of the idea of a white nation. The kid sitting next to me, before class starts, or under his breath after class starts, can go ahead and pledge allegiance to white power if he wants as well. Anybody who does so is a racist bigot, but this is a free country and if somebody wants to be a racist bigot on his own time then the school has nothing to say about it. What I am against is having the teacher start the class with a lesson that involves encouraging the students to adopt bigoted attitudes against those who do not support a white nation."

"See, you're trying to impose your will on everybody else. You want to ban teachers from performing a ritual that a majority of the people here thinks is very important, but which you happen to dislike. You are completely intolerant of any view other than your own, so if a teacher expresses a view that you do not share, you want to ban it."

"Yes, I dislike it," Shawn said. "I don't like having a government teacher standing in front of the class and leading the class in a pledge to white power."

"And you want to force your will on the majority. The majority sees absolutely nothing wrong with a pledge of allegiance to white power. This is a democracy. That's how democracies work. If you don't want to live in a free country I can give you a long list of other countries that you can move to."

"Actually, Mr. Fox, I do not want to force my view on the majority. I want the majority to realize that only racist bigots would support such a proposal, and I want the majority to voluntarily decide not to be a bunch of racist bigots. A morally just white person will realize that black people are entitled to equal respect from their government and would not support such a pledge. I would like to see a majority that supports justice and refuses to support such a pledge." Shawn stood up and added, "Thank you for your time, Mr. Fox. I don't think that you would be a very good advocate."

"Sorry," Fox said. "Good luck."

Just as Shawn stepped into the hallway, another of the guidance councilors, Mr. Reynolds, walked by. Reynolds had helped Shawn get enrolled in the school and pick his classes during the summer. He smiled at seeing Shawn, then the smile faded. "Shawn. I would ask you how things are going, but I hear that they are not going very well."

"I'm in a bit of a jam right now, Mr. Reynolds."

"I'm sorry, Shawn," Reynolds said. "Although, I think it's not exactly fair to hold you responsible for this. It's just that, as you know, white people have a moral sense that black people just don't have. That means that you just don't understand why certain things are wrong the way that we do. The only thing that a black person knows is what pleases him at a given moment. He doesn't see the value of doing things for any reason outside of his own pleasure. For you, this seems like a good idea. But, it's wrong. If you had the moral sense that white people have, you would see that."

"Actually, Mr. Reynolds, I don't think that white people have a special moral sense. White people only have a set of cultural prejudices that turn out to recommend rituals and practices that work to secure white people in positions of power. Black people are just as capable of acting morally as whites – better, in fact, in some instances and worse in others. But it's useful to say that blacks lack a moral sense because that can be used to make sure that blacks are kept down in this society while white people continue to be elevated above them."

Reynolds sighed. "I've always found it frustrating talking to people like you, Shawn. Really, it's a lot like trying to explain the color 'blue' to a blind man. I can see, so the word 'blue' makes perfectly good sense to me. I can see it. I know what it looks like. But you're blind, so how can I get you to understand 'blue'? In this case, I have a moral sense. I can see the rightness and wrongness of things as clearly as I can see the color blue. But you're black. You're morally blind. Somehow, I need to explain to you that some things can be wrong and that you shouldn't pursue them, even though you lack the sense that will allow you to see it for yourself. The blind man, if he is wise, will trust himself to be guided by somebody who can see. You, too, Shawn, need to learn to be guided by those of us who have moral sight. Trust me, Shawn, we have a much better grasp of the difference between right and wrong than you do."

"How do you know this? How do you know that you have a moral sense and I don't? What you call a moral sense is what I could call a different set of prejudices. Of course you want to think that your prejudices have moral power – that way you can force your way on others without guilt. But how do you know this?"

"It's obvious," said Reynolds. "It's evident in the fact that you don't see that it is perfectly legitimate for white people to have a pledge of allegiance to a white nation and I do. Eighty-seven percent of us are white. If that's not enough to justify calling us a white nation and pledging allegiance to a white nation, then I don't know what is."

"So, the reason that you are right on moral issues such as having 'white' in the Pledge of Allegiance is because you have this superior moral sense. And the reason we know that you have this superior moral sense is because you can sense that it is perfectly acceptable to put the word 'white' in the Pledge of Allegiance."

"Well, it's a little more complicated than that, but that's the basic idea," Reynolds said.

"I have no doubt that you believe in your moral superiority over me, Mr. Reynolds. I have no doubt that you believe in your moral sense, even though you have no evidence for it. However, that's a failing on your part, Mr. Reynolds. I have a right that you give me the respect of a moral equal, Mr. Reynolds, unless and until you can prove beyond a reasonable doubt that I am not your moral equal. Anything else makes you a bigot. And when you base your claim to moral superiority on mere faith – on a mere wish that you are morally superior to me – that just compounds your bigotry. So, if you don't mind, I must take my morally depraved carcass back to detention."

Shawn turned to leave, but Reynolds stopped him. "Hold on a moment, Shawn. I have a question."

Pausing, Shawn said, "Okay, what?"

"Okay, you think I'm wrong. You think that there's something wrong with pledging allegiance to a white nation. You think that I am morally blind because I can't see that. Now, in order to condemn me like that, you have to be thinking that you are better than I am. You have to be thinking that it is okay for you to judge me – to look down on me for supporting a pledge of allegiance to a white nation. Yet, you condemn me for thinking that I am better than you. Doesn't that make you a hypocrite? Aren't you condemning me for the same thing that you think is perfectly acceptable for you to do yourself?"

"Mr. Reynolds, let's assume that you just said that you were taller than me. We both know that is not true. You are, I would guess, no more than five foot six, while I am five foot nine. So, I say that your claim to be taller than me is false. Instead, I claim that I am taller than you. That's not hypocrisy, Mr. Reynolds. That's a fact."

"You are saying that your moral superiority is a fact," Reynolds said.

"On this issue – on the issue of having the government encourage students to pledge allegiance to a white nation – I am right and you are wrong. On some other issue, you might be right and I might be wrong. In fact, you might actually be morally superior to me, having more right answers than I do. But this is not one of them."

"But, morally, how can you possibly know that you're right and I am wrong, when I am the one with the moral sense, and you are not?"

"I know that I am right because I know that that the burden of proof is not on those who declare themselves to be innocent, but on those who declare others to be guilty. Your proof relies on this nonsense that you have a moral sense. It's a fiction. It does not overrule the moral obligation to equal treatment in the eyes of the government."

"I stumped you, didn't I?" Reynolds said with a self-satisfied smile. "You don't have an answer for that."

"Good bye. Mr. Reynolds," Shawn said.

"Think about this, Shawn. Just, think about it. You can't refute me. You haven't said anything that actually works against my claim that whites have a moral sense. You have only asserted that you do not believe it. However, even though you can't refute my views, you want to sweep them aside."

"Consider your views refuted, Mr. Reynolds. Good day."

Basking in self-congratulation, Mr. Reynolds continued on to his office.

11. The Hearing

Superintendant Brad Thomson called the administrative hearing into session.

There was no official location for this type of meeting; the administrators simply took over an empty classroom for a couple of hours. Three administrators, presiding over the meeting, sat in three comfortable office chairs that had been rolled into the room and set behind a collapsible table. Principal Hadley set up his station at the teacher's desk, while Shawn was invited to take one of the student's seats. His mother sat quietly at the back of the room in one corner while Ms. Shelby Johnson stood in the back near the other corner.

The night before, Shawn had asked his mother not to interfere in the hearing. He said that he knew that the administrators were going to decide against him, and that there was nothing he could do about that – or, more precisely, he was not willing to do any of the things he could do. So, at the hearing, Shawn's mom sat and fiddled with the strap to her purse while she listened to the hearing.

Superintendent Thomson announced, "Shawn Henry, I assume that you have been given a copy of Principal Hadley's argument as to why you should be removed from this school. According to Mr. Hadley, you insist on disrupting class by pledging allegiance to 'one black nation' after the rest of the students give the proper pledge of allegiance. Of course, we cannot allow students to disrupt class. Is it true that you insist on this disruption?"

"No, sir," Shawn answered.

Superintendant Thomson folded his hands on the desk. "Would you mind explaining that answer?"

"I have a question first, sir." Shawn said.

"Go ahead."

"When the rest of the class stands and pledges allegiance to a white nation, and I sit in my desk patiently waiting for them to finish, are they guilty of causing a disruption?"

"That's not the same thing!" Hadley shouted, rising out of his chair.

Thomson waved Hadley back. "You'll have your turn, Principal Hadley."

"That's my question, Mr. Thomson," Shawn said. "If the school can have a rule in which the rest of the class stands and pledges allegiance to a white nation while others sit quietly, then the school can have a rule in which those who stood during the standard pledge can remain silently seated while others, if they want, pledge allegiance to one black nation. If the first pledge is not a disruption, then the second should not be a disruption either."

Thomson grunted, "And are we to require that each student who has their own favorite version of the pledge be given time as well? I would ask you, Mr. Henry, when do you expect to actually have time to hold class?"

"No, sir. I think it is absolutely true that a patriotic Amerycan will support liberty and justice for all. If somebody wants to pledge allegiance to tyranny and injustice, then they are simply wrong to do so. The school has no need to allow equal time to such an absurdity. It's just as absurd to have a student pledge allegiance to rebellion. It is a contradiction to be loyal to this government and to support a rebellion against it. But it is also absurd, as a matter of fact, to claim that a patriot must support a white nation in the same way he must support union, liberty, and justice for all."

"Mr. Henry, state law requires that students start each day with the Pledge of Allegiance."

"That law is being obeyed in what I suggested, Mr. Thomson. I stand. I pledge allegiance to the flag. Mr. Hadley says that this is a disturbance, but I am doing the same thing that the other students have just finished doing, and nobody calls their action a disturbance."

"Yet, you pledge allegiance to a black nation, Mr. Henry," Thomson said.

"And the rest of the students are pledging allegiance to a white nation. I would be more than happy to have a single pledge of allegiance if we are pledging to one nation with liberty and justice for all. However, since the government has decided to divide our country between those who support white power and those who do not, then it seems we need two pledges of allegiance; one for those who believe in a white nation and one for those that do not."

"None of that matters, Mr. Henry. The ceremony requires that the students use the one and only Pledge of Allegiance that bears the government's approval. Your outburst is clearly not a part of the official ceremony. If you were in a chorus, Mr. Henry, and you wait for everybody else to finish the song that is in the program, then you insist on singing your own song after they are done, then I hope even you can understand why you would be removed from that chorus. If you wish to pledge allegiance to the flag, which I think any good Amerycan citizen would do, then you can do so at the same time and using the same pledge as everybody else. If you do not wish to show your patriotism by saying the Pledge of Allegiance, then you may remain seated and remain silent. You may not disrupt the chorus by standing up and giving your solo performance because you don't like the director's arrangement."

"There is an important difference between this situation and a chorus, Mr. Thomson. With the Pledge of Allegiance, the government officially declares that people like me and my father are not fit to be counted among the group of patriotic Americans. It's not a song, sir. It is a pledge. In this case, it is a pledge to view people like me and my father, who do not support a white nation, to be like those who do not support union, liberty, and justice for all."

"I'm sorry to hear about your father, Mr. Henry, but his sacrifice, however noble, is not relevant to this case. This case concerns whether or not you insist on disrupting a class by stating an unapproved pledge out of turn with the rest of the class."

Shawn stepped around to the front of the table. "I don't see that as the real question, Mr. Thomson. I think that the real question is whether a teacher has the right to stand in front of a class and denigrate her students on the basis of nothing more than the unreasoned prejudice of the majority. Clearly, when we pledge allegiance to one nation with liberty and justice for all, we are supposed to understand this to be a statement that denigrates and degrades anybody who would support tyranny and injustice. And when we pledge allegiance to one nation indivisible we are, in a sense, giving the finger to anyone who would support a rebellion. So, when we pledge allegiance to a white nation, the school and the government itself is teaching its students that good Amerycans will view those who do not support a white nation with the same disrespect. The real question is whether the school has a right to teach the students sent there to adopt this bigotry against fellow citizens who do not deserve it."

"That is a question for the legislators to decide, and the legislature has decided. Your teacher is doing what the law requires, Mr. Henry. If you have a complaint, you should take it up with the government."

"Mr. Hadley suggested that option, Mr. Thomson," Shawn said. "However, I assume that you are aware that the government is made up entirely of white people. These white people are elected by the citizens. Those citizens have spent twelve years going through a public school system where they have been told to pledge allegiance to white power. I do not think that it is a viable option."

"Your political problems do not argue for your right to disrupt class with your personal, private, political protest, Mr. Henry. We have no obligation to provide you with a soap box and a captive audience during class time. In fact, we have an obligation to prevent you from interfering with our mission to use class time for classroom instruction."

"Yes, but you do not have an obligation to use class time to teach your students to be bigots. In fact, the opposite is true. Spend that time teaching students something other than bigotry, Mr. Thomson, and the country will be better for it."

Principal Hadley suddenly stood and shouted, "The legislature has every right to make sure that students learn patriotism along with math, science, and grammar. Patriotism is an important lesson, and we will, in fact, teach our students to be patriotic Amerycans even if the legislature did not require it."

Shawn answered, "The only way the Pledge, in its current form, can be considered patriotic is if we accept the assumption that patriots must support a white nation, and those who do not support a white nation cannot be patriots."

"Yes, Shawn. Patriots support a white nation. People who do not support a white nation are not patriots. Is it even possible for anything to be more obvious? All of our founding fathers were white. Eighty-seven percent of Amerycans are white. Ameryca is a white nation. Open your eyes. Look around you. You are surrounded by white people. That's a fact. If you are not pledging allegiance to a white nation, then you are not pledging allegiance to Ameryca. It is as simple as that."

"Enough," said Thomson. "The purpose of this hearing is not to discuss the merits of the Pledge of Allegiance. We are not here to overrule the legislature, we are here to obey the legislature. The legislature requires time to say the Pledge of Allegiance, and that is what we do. The legislature requires that the rest of the class period be devoted to classroom instruction, and that is also what we do. If the legislature sets aside a minute at the start of each class for student political speeches, then we will obey that law as well. However, it has not done so. The law we have today, Mr. Henry, says that you will either participate in the nationally recognized Pledge of Allegiance to one white nation, indivisible, with liberty and justice for all, or sit quietly while the rest of the class does so. Are you prepared to follow those requirements?"

"The legislature has no right to have students pledging allegiance to white power," Shawn repeated.

"I repeat, that is irrelevant, Mr. Henry. If you have nothing new to add, we ask that you clear the room while we discuss our decision. We will summon you when we are ready. Don't go very far, I don't think that this will take long."

Shawn rose, gathered his books, and walked to the back of the room. There, he took his mother's arm and walked out with her. Professor Hadley was close behind. He moved a short distance down the hall and took out his cell phone to place a call. Ms. Johnson stood by herself as well, leaning against the wall, with her arms folded in front of her.

As promised, it took only a few minutes for the committee to summon them back into the room. Superintendent Thomson called Shawn before the table and said, "This wasn't even worth our time to debate, Mr. Henry. Clearly you intend to disrupt class. Clearly, we cannot allow that. If you cannot attend class without disruption, then you may not attend class. You may, if you wish, apply for readmission next semester. We will be happy to have you back. However, your readmission will be contingent on exactly the same conditions that I have set before you today. It requires your personal commitment not to disrupt class with your silly demonstrations. You are hereby expelled. You may clean out your locker."

At the end of the speech, Thomson handed over a copy of the expulsion order, which the three administrators had all signed and dated. They then stood and left the room. Principal Hadley left with them, chatting happily about how they had made the right decision.

Shawn turned and saw his mom still sitting, holding a tissue to her eyes. He also noticed Ms. Johnson, standing motionless. Shawn struggled to think of something to say, but he could not. He simply picked up his backpack and walked back to his mom. He told the guard that he did not need to go back to his locker, since he had already packed the last of his belongings into his backpack. Together with his mom, he left the building

12. Aftermath

Monday came, and Shelby Johnson was amazed to think that this was only the second week of school. The first week had seemed unending. When the bell rang, she looked out over her class and focused on the two empty desks – the desk that Shawn had occupied near the back by the door, and the desk where Jenny had sat nearer the middle of the room.

Students entering the room congratulated each other on Shawn's expulsion. The news had gone through the school after Ms. Johnson's history class had ended on Friday, so this was the first time the students had an opportunity to celebrate this victory as a group.

At the sound of the bell, the students took their seats, seemingly eager to start the new day.

Shelby leaned back against the front of her desk and took a deep breath.

"We are not going to say the Pledge of Allegiance in this class today," she announced. "In fact, I will never again lead any class in the Pledge of Allegiance as it is currently written."

The class was stunned into silence. Shelby did not think that she could have done a better job of getting their undivided attention.

"Shawn Henry was right. If I tell you that being a loyal Amerycan means supporting a white nation, I'm telling you that we have no room in this country for black people except insofar as they serve a white nation. I would be telling you to look down on fellow citizens and classmates that the government has no business telling you to look down on."

She had rehearsed her speech all weekend, and it flowed smoothly. "I have no trouble asking you to pledge allegiance to liberty and justice for all. When I do so, I am telling you that there is no room in this country for anybody who would support tyranny and injustice. We don't want them in this country. We also don't want people in this country who would support another civil war. In this class we will cover Amerycan history up through the civil war, and you will see why we don't want to go through another one of those.

"This means that if I were also to tell you to pledge allegiance to a white nation, I'm saying that we have no room in this country for those who do not think that this needs to be a white nation. This is in direct conflict with the idea that people of all races have a right to be given equal respect in the eyes of their government. The government is not giving equal respect when it has its students pledging to the superiority of one group over another."

Shelby paused for a moment to let the students think about those words. One of the students raised her hand, but Shelby ignored her for the time being. "One of the things that this means is that I might not be here very much longer. I think that Mr. Hadley will be as upset about my decision to break the rules that require a Pledge of Allegiance to a white nation as he was about Shawn and Jenny. There is nothing that I have ever wanted in the world more than being a teacher. Nobody makes a more important contribution to the future of this country than teachers. This was a very hard decision for me to make. However, Jenny had said that a good person isn't necessarily the person who makes the right decision when it is easy. She's somebody who makes the right decision when it is hard."

The speech was over. Shelby took a deep breath. She had pulled the trigger and she had nothing to do but to wait for the score. Except, she had some time to try to teach a room full of students a little bit of Amerycan History. She pointed to the student who had raised her hand. "Andie, if your question is about the Pledge of Allegiance, I have said everything I intend to say on that issue. If it's about Amerycan History and our assignment for this week, go ahead and ask it."

Andie lowered her hand and shook her head.

"Okay," said Shelby, "Then let's continue with our discussion of the Age of Discovery."

Appendix A: "In God We Trust"

To understand the problem with having a national motto of 'In God We Trust," we merely need to look at other mottos and what they mean.

For example, the Marine Corps uses the motto, *Semper Fidelis* (often abbreviated as *Semper Fi*), which means 'always faithful' The purpose of this motto is to identify one of the most important values for anybody who deserves to be called a Marine. It is not merely a description that, 'It happens to be the case that most Marines are faithful to their comrades in arms.' It says, 'A good Marine is one who is faithful to his comrades in arms, and any Marine who is not faithful to his comrades in arms falls short of what it means to be a Marine.' In fact, a Marine who is not faithful to his comrades in arms is not worthy of the name.

The same is true of the Boy Scout motto, *Be Prepared.* Nobody thinks that all Boy Scouts actually are prepared at all times. The motto represents an ideal – something that all Boy Scouts are to strive for. Those who succeed are considered better Boy Scouts than those who fail. A Boy Scout who is not prepared, or who can be criticized for his lack of preparedness, is expected to feel shame at his short-comings, and to try harder in the future.

So, when the United States government adopted as the motto, *In God We Trust* in 1956, it established the same type of standard for the nation that *Semper Fi* established for the Marine Corps and *Be Prepared* established for the Boy Scouts. The motto means that trusting in God is something that all Americans should strive for. Those who succeed (to the degree that they succeed) are good Americans who should feel proud in the same way that Boy Scouts who are prepared should feel proud.

At the same time, the motto says that those who fail to trust in God should feel shame or guilt for their short-comings. Indeed, it says that an American who does not trust in God is like a Marine not faithful to his comrades in arms. He is somebody that other Americans should look down on – somebody not worthy of the name 'American'.

This, of course, is something that the government has no right to say about citizens who are as law-abiding and patriotic as any other, but who believe that the type of god we should 'trust' almost certainly does not exist.

The claim that this motto makes is not only false, it is malicious. It establishes a national policy of promoting the condemnation of good citizens. It is sensible to condemn a Marine not faithful to his comrades in arms, and sensible to teach children the value of being prepared. It is not sensible, and it is certainly not right, to teach a nation – particularly to teach young children who cannot question what they are being taught – to look down on neighbors who are as good and loyal as any other but who do not trust in God.

Some people claim that 'In God We Trust' has fallen into the realm of 'ceremonial deism' and that it has lost its prescriptive force.

However, I would like anybody who believes this to go up to a Marine and say that *Semper Fidelis* is merely a ceremonial motto that has lost its prescriptive force. If it had, in fact, lost its prescriptive force, then it no longer serves as a worthy motto. It should be discarded and replaced with something else – something that Marines should strive for. As a matter of fact, we do not need to replace this motto because, among Marines *Semper Fidelis* still makes an important statement about what a Marine *should* be.

Or tell a troop of Boy Scouts that *be prepared* is merely a ceremonial slogan and that they should not actually take this to mean that there is anything good to be said about being prepared.

If it is the case that "In God We Trust" has lost its prescriptive force, then we need to reject the motto and find a new one. It should be a motto that identifies a value that Americans should actually strive for – one that actually does distinguish a good American worthy of the name from those that fall short of the ideal American.

The national motto that our founding fathers adopted was, *e pluribus unum* (from many, one). It was a motto that held forth the ideal of Americans working together as one. Originally, it meant many states coming together to form a new nation. However, it can easily be taken to mean a group of diverse citizens coming together to form one nation.

The new (1956, 'In God We Trust') motto is actually a blatant contradiction of the motto that the founding fathers adopted. Instead of telling us to come together, it tells us that we are to think of ourselves as separate groups – a 'we' or 'included' or 'American' group who 'trusts in God' and, of course, a 'they' or 'outsider' or 'un-American' group that does not.

I want to point out that I am making no explicit argument here based on the Constitution of the United States. Even where no such Constitution exists, it would be wrong for the government to adopt a motto that divides its people into 'we' and 'they' as this one does. Even where no Constitutional prohibition on establishing a religion exists, it would be wrong for the government to denigrate citizens who do not trust in God by declaring that they fail to live up to the American ideal of trusting in God. Private citizens, of course, are free to make such a statement – however wrong and bigoted it may be. However, the government has no right to make such a statement about loyal and law-abiding citizens.

There is a sense in which it would have been easy to include some discussion of the motto 'In God We Trust' in the context of this story. After all, "In God We Trust" is an inherently segregationist slogan that conceptually divides the nation between a 'we' group (who trusts in God) and a 'they' group (who do not). Any segregationist sign in the context of the story – such as signs that distinguish between 'white' and 'colored' bathrooms or drinking fountains or schools would serve the same function in Ameryca that 'In God We Trust' does in America.

For example, in Ameryca, a sign that says "White Power" would have been a good representation of the segregationist nature of a sign that says, "In God We Trust" – since the latter effectively says, "Power to Those who Trust in God."

Principal Hadley returned to this desk. He had a stack of mail waiting for him, but it took him a while to calm down enough that he could actually focus on what he saw. He first sorted through the mail, picking out those that looked the most interesting or important and dropping them onto the desk in front of him.

One of the letters in the stack was from an organization, "WhitePower-Ameryca.org." Curious as to what this letter might say, he dropped the rest of the mail and tore it open.

Their mission, as stated at the very top of the letter, was "To promote patriotism by encouraging elected officials to display our national motto of 'White Power' in every classroom in Ameryca."

Hadley immediately liked the idea. When he looked for a price, he discovered that various donors from around the country were putting up the money to make and ship a decorative sign with the motto – a decorative 8" by 10" picture of the Amerycan flag with the words, 'White Power' boldly printed on the front of it.

We can then imagine how it would have been for Shawn to enter into his expulsion hearing, having the meeting start with the Pledge of Allegiance to 'one white nation', seeing a sign behind the heads of the administrators that had the words 'white power' printed over an image of the Amerycan flag, wondering whether he had any chance to convince them that promoting a white Ameryca was not a morally permissible action.

A national motto identifies a value that all good Americans can strive for. A national motto says that any American who does not strive for this value is not a good American. When a nation adopts a motto that excludes law-abiding, patriotic citizens, the nation has adopted bigotry as a core value. No fair and just people would do such a thing.

Appendix B: Offense and Freedom of Speech

Nothing that I have written in this book should be interpreted as a claim that a statement may be condemned merely because the listener or reader finds it offensive. A person who is not potentially offended by what he may read or hear is a person who does not live in a free society. A person who insists that offensive statements be barred is a person who insists that freedom be curtailed.

The criterion by which statements should be evaluated is not by whether or not the person finds it offensive, but by whether the statement is true or false. If an offensive statement is true, then the offended party needs to learn how to live with that truth, regardless of how offensive she might find it. If the offensive statement is false, then it may be condemned. However, it is not to be condemned because it is offensive. It is to be condemned because it is false, and the person who condemns it needs to provide reason to believe that it is false.

When a person makes a false statement we can ask whether that error is a morally culpable error – an error that shows that the speaker or writer has an important flaw in his or her character. We do this by answering the question, "What would have caused the person to make this particular mistake?"

If we can trace the error back to some defect in character, then we can say of the person that, "You are not only wrong in this matter, your error shows you to be a contemptible individual. No good person would have made such an error." If the error does not show a defect in character, we have no reason to add condemnation to our accusation that the speaker or writer has made a mistake. We simply point out the mistake and move on.

An example of a non-culpable error is one in which a mother, following the advice of a doctor, gives her child something that she thinks will cure the child's illness. If the medicine ends up making the child sicker – even killing him, this was not the mother's fault. She had good reason for her belief – she had acquired that belief the way that morally responsible people acquire their beliefs. We cannot blame her for killing the child – it was an accident.

An example of a culpable error is one in which the mother, following the advice of her brother who has never been known for being particularly bright, gives her child something that she thinks will cure the child's illness. In this case, if the medicine poisons the child, we actually have good reason to blame the mother for her actions.

She was careless. A morally responsible parent would have acted differently with such poorly supported information. A mother who truly cares about the welfare of her child would have sought a second, better informed opinion before she acted. The mere fact that the mother did not take steps to avoid a potentially fatal error tells us that she did not actually care about the possibility of making a fatal mistake. That is where she shows the flaw in her moral character. It tells us that she lacks the qualities that a good and morally responsible person would have, to make sure that beliefs that might cause her to act in ways harmful to others have a more solid footing.

A second type of morally culpable error is one in which the agent embraces an error because she wants to, and she wants to because she is full of hate and needs a reason to think that her hate is legitimate. The emails being circulated during the 2008 Presidential campaign that says that Barak Obama turns his back on the flag during the Pledge of Allegiance and took his oath of office on the Koran are examples of this attitude. People who believed these claims showed that they were full of hate for Obama and wanted only to find a reason to make that hate seem legitimate. When they heard these stories, they said to themselves, "This sounds like a good reason to hate Obama, so the stories must be true." They let their hate select their evidence.

In putting 'under God' in the Pledge of Allegiance and changing the national motto to 'In God We Trust' the American government made itself guilty of the moral crime of promoting a malicious falsehoods against good citizens. It promotes the falsehood that an American who is not 'under God' is as un-American as one who supports rebellion, tyranny, or injustice. It promotes the falsehood that an American who falls short of the ideal of trusting in God is undeserving of the name 'American,' in the same way that a Marine who falls short of the Marine motto *Semper Fi* is unworthy of being called a Marine.

These denigrating and derogatory statements about citizens who do not believe in God are lies. Furthermore, they are the types of lies that are motivated by malicious intent. They are the types of lies that are adopted by people who say, "I need a reason to hate these people. This lie that they are not good Americans would be a good reason to hate them if it were true, so it must be true."

This type of reasoning is not just offensive, and it is not to be condemned merely for the flaw of being offensive. It is malicious falsehood. It is bigotry in its purist form.

Anybody who claims that my arguments are meant to show that a pledge of allegiance to 'one nation under God' or a national motto of 'In God We Trust' are morally illegitimate because they are offensive has not understood what I have written. The problem is not that they are offensive. The problem is that they are malicious errors – errors motivated by hatred and prejudice – by a desire to hate that motivates agents to adopt whatever appears to wrap their prejudice in an illusion of legitimacy.

And if anybody objects to what I have written because they find it offensive, my response is that this is not morally relevant. If one has an objection to what I have written they need to first demonstrate that I have made a mistake. After that, they must provide evidence that my mistake was either the result of negligence or maliciousness on my part. Without this evidence, their 'offense' is not a legitimate concern.

Another important concept that I want to look at is the right to freedom of speech. Here I am not talking about the legal right, but the moral right – the right from which just law gets its legitimacy.

The moral right to freedom of speech is not a right to be free from criticism. Criticism is also speech. The person who says that we must preserve freedom of speech by banning criticism is like a person who says that we must preserve a building by burning it to the ground. His words are nonsense.

The right to freedom of speech means that a person may speak without fear of physical violence – including the physical violence inherent in government actions. The right to freedom of speech means that the only legitimate response to words are words and private actions. Private actions are those actions that one may perform without justifying them to anybody. They include decisions about such things as where to shop, what to buy, what to listen to, who to vote for, who to invite over for dinner, where to visit, where to make charitable donations. A society that embraces freedom of speech recognizes the legitimacy of all of these types of responses. It denies that legitimacy of violence as a response.

Any who respond to words (or drawings, or cartoons, or any attempt to communicate) with violence or threats of violence proves by their actions that they have no love of freedom. They prove themselves to be enemies of freedom because, by these very actions, they are demanding that speakers and writers be made less free.

I am not violating the right to freedom of speech of those who would promote 'one nation under God' and a motto of 'In God We Trust' by criticizing them. I am not in any way advocating that we respond to words with violence. They have as much right to argue for the conceptual segregation of Americans into groups that trust in God and those who do not as the KKK has to argue for the physical segregation of the races. They have just as much right to make these types of claims – and they are just as morally contemptible for doing so.

The right to freedom of speech that allows them to say such things without fear of violence is the same right to freedom of speech that allows others to criticize them for their malicious hate-motivated bigotry also without fear of violence.

Respecting this right is one way that a person can show his respect for the principle of liberty and justice for all.

www.ingramcontent.com/pod-product-compliance
Lightning Source LLC
LaVergne TN
LVHW091206080426
835509LV00006B/861

9780615200774